Introductory Level

Read and Reflect

Academic Reading Strategies and Cultural Awareness

Series Editors:
Lori Howard
Jayme Adelson-Goldstein

ESL CENTER

OXFORD
UNIVERSITY PRESS

OXFORD
UNIVERSITY PRESS

198 Madison Avenue
New York, NY 10016 USA

Great Clarendon Street, Oxford OX2 6DP UK

Oxford University Press is a department of the University of Oxford.
It furthers the University's objective of excellence in research, scholarship,
and education by publishing worldwide in

Oxford New York

Auckland Cape Town Dar es Salaam Hong Kong Karachi
Kuala Lumpur Madrid Melbourne Mexico City Nairobi
New Delhi Shanghai Taipei Toronto

With offices in

Argentina Austria Brazil Chile Czech Republic France Greece
Guatemala Hungary Italy Japan Poland Portugal Singapore
South Korea Switzerland Thailand Turkey Ukraine Vietnam

OXFORD and OXFORD ENGLISH are registered trademarks of
Oxford University Press

Library of Congress Cataloging-in-Publication Data

Read and reflect, introductory level: academic reading strategies and cultural
awareness.
    p. cm.
    Includes bibliographical references.
    ISBN-13: 978-0-19-437731-7 (pbk.)
    ISBN-10: 0-19-437731-8
    1. English language—Textbooks for foreign speakers. 2. Reading
comprehension—Problems, exercises, etc. 3. College readers.
PE1128.R385 2006
428.6'4—dc22   2005018030

No unauthorized photocopying

Executive Publisher: Janet Aitchison

Senior Acquisitions Editor: Pietro Alongi

Editor: Dena Daniel

Associate Editor: Scott Allan Wallick

Art Director: Maj-Britt Hagsted

Senior Designer: Claudia Carlson

Senior Art Editor: Judi DeSouter

Art Editor: Justine Eun

Production Manager: Shanta Persaud

Production Controller: Eve Wong

ISBN-13: 978 0 19 4377317
ISBN-10: 0 19 4377318

Printed in Hong Kong

10 9 8 7 6 5 4 3 2 1

ACKNOWLEDGMENTS

Illustrations: Paul Hampson pp. 1, 8, 17, 33, 49, 65, 72, 81, 83, 104;
Michael Hortens pp. 2, 90, 108, 113; Jon Keegan pp. 5, 35, 44, 57, 61, 62,
66 (fashion), 82, 92, 115; William Waitzman pp. 7, 12, 24, 41, 53, 58, 66
(drugstore scene), 76, 98, 120.

*The publisher would like to thank the following for their permission to reproduce
photographs and cartoons:* Bananastock/Punchstock pp. 10, 21 (two-way
communication); Peter Beavis/Taxi/Getty Images p. 69 (natural model);
Bettmann/CORBIS p. 34 ('Ben the Luggage Boy' cover); Big Cheese
Photo/Punchstock p. 19; Blend Images/Punchstock p. 105; Brand X
Pictures p. 74; David Brownell p. 3; Charles O. Cecil p. 93; CORBIS p.
34 ('Ragged Dick' cover); Photo courtesy of DARTS, www.darts1.org
p. 13; Kay Hinton/Emory Magazine p. 14; Mark E. Gibson p. 85
(wilderness camping); The Granger Collection, New York pp. 37, 69
(Gibson Girl); Randall Hyman p. 18; The Kobal Collection pp. 69 (Doris
Day), 108; Dennis MacDonald/Alamy p. 42 (job interview); The New
Yorker Collection 1989 Charles Barsotti from cartoonbank.com. All
Rights Reserved p. 38; Omni-Photo Communications p. 50; David
Parket/Omni-Photo Communications p. 122; Photodisc/Punchstock
p. 21 (one-way communication); Photri-Microstock p. 85 (RV camping);
Courtesy of the Rolling Dog Ranch Animal Sanctuary p. 94; Photo
courtesy of St. John's University p. 45; Stock Image/Imagestate p. 74
(woman); Graeme Teague/GTPHOTO p. 124; Thinkstock/Punchstock
p. 46; David Young-Wolff/Alamy p. 42 (woman researching).

*The publisher would like to thank the following for their permission to adapt and
reproduce copyright material:* p. 13 "Tianna Bailey Helps Kids" by Paige P.
Parvin, used by permission of Emory Magazine; p. 14 "Senior Helps
Seniors" used by permission of DARTS, www.darts1.org.

Introduction

Welcome to *Read and Reflect: Academic Reading Strategies and Cultural Awareness*

This reading series for beginning and intermediate students of English as a second or foreign language has four key goals:

- to develop students' awareness and use of reading strategies
- to increase their academic vocabulary, thus preparing them to read academic texts
- to provide a forum for students to learn about and discuss aspects of American culture
- to increase students' enjoyment of the reading process through a wealth of high-interest texts

This book is ideal for young adults planning to pursue a college education; however, it can also be used by students who want to improve their reading skills to attain a personal goal or to advance in the workplace.

Read and Reflect teaches students to read with purpose and comprehension and to interact with the text as they read. In each unit of *Read and Reflect*, students are introduced to a new strategy that supports the target reading skill (for example, looking at the title and pictures in a text is a strategy for previewing). Exercises throughout the book have students apply these strategies as they read. Activities in all levels help students develop reading fluency. Level 2 also has specific exercises to develop reading speed.

How This Book Is Organized

Read and Reflect contains eight thematic units, each tied to a cultural concept such as happiness, family communication, and the effects of television. To maximize reading opportunities, each unit contains four texts adapted from authentic sources. These texts have different topics, but are connected to the overall cultural theme. Cartoons, questionnaires, charts, and narrative paragraphs provide additional reading practice.

At the beginning of each unit, the cultural theme and reading goals are introduced. Students are asked what they know about the theme and then discuss their prior knowledge, thoughts, and ideas. Pre-reading activities throughout the book provide background information, key vocabulary, and critical reading strategies that enhance students' comprehension of the texts.

All texts are followed by processing activities that require students to demonstrate their understanding, and to use their higher-level thinking skills to analyze and synthesize new information. Because active vocabulary development is an important part of developing reading proficiency, vocabulary exercises occur throughout the units.

A key feature of each unit is the Read and Share activity. Students read one of two parts of the same text in order to share and discuss what they learned. This activity gives students an enhanced purpose for reading while also providing them with an opportunity to apply the reading strategies they have learned.

At the end of each unit, students reflect on the theme of the unit and what they have read about it. First they read a short, personal narrative on the theme and then, using it as a model, write their own paragraph.

Special Features of this Series

- Academic reading strategies
- Academic vocabulary
- Reading skills and vocabulary recycled from unit to unit
- Adapted authentic materials
- Strategies to improve reading speed
- Collaborative learning opportunities
- Critical literacy development

A more detailed description of these features and the unit activities is included in the Teacher's Notes on page 135. The Answer Key begins on page 129.

We hope you find *Read and Reflect* a useful and enjoyable teaching tool. We welcome your comments and ideas. Please write to us care of:
Oxford University Press
English Language Teaching Division
198 Madison Avenue
New York, New York 10016

Jayme Adelson-Goldstein and Lori Howard

Contents

Cultural Concept	Reading Skill	Vocabulary Objective
Happiness	**Previewing:** Preview title, pictures, and captions to determine what you already know about a text.	Comparing with adjectives.
Communication	**Predicting:** After previewing, ask prediction questions about what you will learn from the text.	Use the suffixes *-tion/-sion*.
Personal success	**Connecting Pronouns to Nouns:** Connect pronouns to nouns to help you understand a text.	Identify nouns, verbs, and adjectives in word families.
Anger management	**Understanding Vocabulary in Context:** Look at the words around an unknown word to figure out its meaning.	Use the suffix *-ful*.
Appearance	**Previewing Headings:** Preview headings to give you information about the parts of a text.	Use context clues to understand unknown vocabulary.
Lifestyle	**Previewing Comprehension Questions:** Preview comprehension questions to get information about the important points in the text.	Use context clues to understand unknown vocabulary.
Entertainment	**Asking Questions While You Read:** Ask yourself questions to help you make predictions.	Identify nouns and adjectives in word families.
Housing	**Scanning:** Use numbers and capital letters to help you scan for information in a text.	Use verb phrases.

To the Student

Dear Student,

Welcome to *Read and Reflect*. This series will help you improve your reading in English.

There are 32 texts in this book. These texts come from newspapers, magazines, textbooks, brochures, web sites, and message boards.

In *Read and Reflect* you will:

- read about **many different topics**
- learn **reading skills**
- learn **vocabulary**
- discuss **culture**

Each time you read a text in *Read and Reflect* you will follow these steps:

Get Ready to Read
- Think about the topic.
- Look the title and the pictures.
- Ask yourself, *"What is the reading about?"*

Read
- Read silently.
- Skip over difficult vocabulary words.

Understand the Reading
- Answer the comprehension questions.
- Ask yourself, *"What do I know now?"*

Remember: Practice your new reading skills every time you read. Read often. The more you read, the better and faster you will read!

We wish you good books, good health, and good times.

Lori Howard and Jayme Adelson-Goldstein

ESL CENTER

Unit 1

Finding Happiness

In this unit, you are going to:
- read about happiness in the U.S.
- learn how to preview

WHAT MAKES PEOPLE HAPPY?

A. Look at the picture. What makes these people happy? Discuss your answers with your classmates.

B. What times of life are very happy? Why? Choose two very happy times and mark them with an X. Discuss your answers with your classmates.

___ infancy (ages 0–3)   ___ young adulthood (ages 20–34)

___ childhood (ages 4–12)   ___ middle age (ages 35–54)

___ the teenage years (ages 4–12) ___ the senior years (age 55 and over)

1 GET READY TO READ ABOUT: Happiness And Money

Read the chart. Then complete the sentences with words from the box. Use each word one time.

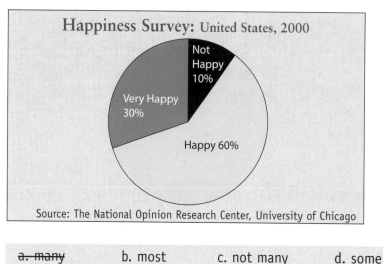

Happiness Survey: United States, 2000

Not Happy 10%

Very Happy 30%

Happy 60%

Source: The National Opinion Research Center, University of Chicago

a. many	b. most	c. not many	d. some

How happy are people in the U.S.? _a_ people are happy. ___ people are very
                              1   2
happy. How many people are not happy? The answer is: ___ people. ___ people (90%) are
                                                      3   4
happy or very happy.

2 BUILD YOUR READING SKILLS: Previewing

Introduction

A. Look at these magazines. Which magazine do you want to read?

B. Think about your choice. Why do you want to read that magazine? Discuss your
   answer with a partner.

Reading Skill

Previewing means looking at a text before you read it. Look at the title. Look at the pictures and charts. Also look at the **captions**—the words under the pictures and charts. Previewing gives you important information.

Practice Previewing

Preview this article. Answer the questions below.

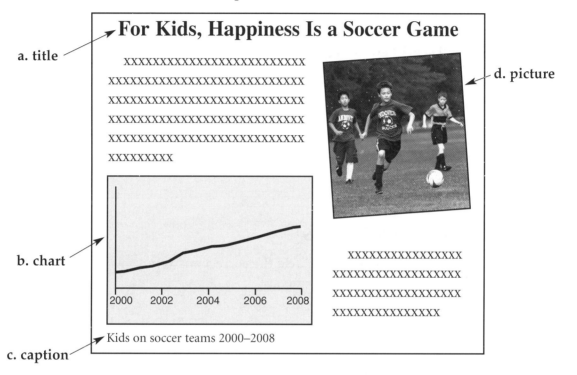

a. title

For Kids, Happiness Is a Soccer Game

d. picture

b. chart

c. caption

Kids on soccer teams 2000–2008

1. What is the title of the article? _____

2. What does the picture show? _____

3. What information do the chart and caption give you? Circle one answer.
   a. more kids play soccer now
   b. more kids like sports now
   c. more kids watch sports now

4. What is this article about? Circle one answer.
   a. soccer for children
   b. famous soccer players
   c. more people to go to soccer games

3 WORDS YOU NEED

Read these new words and their definitions. Then complete the paragraph below with the new words.

> **a. expert:** a person with a lot of knowledge about one topic
>
> **b. do research:** to learn or get information about something
>
> **c. survey:** a list of questions about a topic
>
> **d. compares:** to find similarities and differences
>
> **e. agree:** to have the same opinion

Dr. Ed Diener knows a lot about happiness. He is an ___expert___ on the topic.
1
Diener has some new ideas about happiness. He thinks, "Are they good ideas?"

He needs to _____, or find out more about people's opinions on happiness.
2
First, he uses a _____ and asks people many questions. Then he _____
3   4
people's answers. Sometimes, the groups of people _____, but sometimes
5
they have different opinions.

4 USE YOUR READING SKILLS

Preview the article on page 5. Circle the correct answers.

1. Look at the title. This article is about ____.

    a. money in the U.S.

    b. happiness and money in the U.S.

    c. money in the U.S. and other countries

2. Look at the pictures, chart, and captions. This article has information about ____.

    a. changes from 1950 to the present

    b. the history of U.S. money

    c. TVs and dishwashers

This newspaper article is about two surveys on happiness.

Happiness in the United States: How Important Is Money?

Life in the United States in the 1950s was very different from life today. Dishwashers, televisions, washing machines, and dryers were very new. These appliances were not part of

An American in the 1950s

most families' lives. In the 1950s, a television was a luxury.[1]

Today, most families in the United States have dishwashers, washing machines, dryers, and many other things. Many people are wealthier: They make more money and have more buying power. For example, a simple TV is not ex-

An American today

pensive now, so most people today can buy it.

In many ways, life is much better today—but are people happier? The answer is no. In a survey from 1957, 36% of people were very happy. Almost fifty years later, that number is lower—only 30% of people are very happy.

People today have more money and more things, but they aren't happier. What does this mean? More money does not make people happier. To experts, this is a very interesting idea.

Psychologist[2] Ed Diener is researching this idea.

Diener compares two groups. The people in one group are from a list of very wealthy people. The people in the other group are from a phone book. They are ordinary people — not rich and not poor. Diener's results are interesting: very wealthy people are happier, but only a little happier.

Of course,[3] people need money to live, but more money doesn't mean more happiness. Experts agree: Money can't buy happiness.

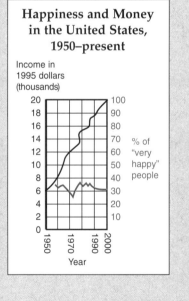

Happiness and Money in the United States, 1950–present

Income in 1995 dollars (thousands)

% of "very happy" people

[1] **luxury:** an expensive and nice thing
[2] **psychologist:** an expert on the ways people think and act
[3] **of course:** certainly; it is true

6 UNDERSTAND THE READING

A. Circle the correct answer.

1. Compare the 1950s and today. Most Americans today have ____ .
   a. less money
   b. the same money
   c. more money

2. Compare the 1950s and today. Most Americans today are ____ .
   a. a little less happy
   b. a little happier
   c. a lot happier

3. Psychologist Ed Diener compares ____ .
   a. people in the 1950s and people today
   b. very wealthy people and ordinary people
   c. people in the U.S. and people in other countries

4. Diener's results are interesting: very wealthy people ____ .
   a. are only a little happier than ordinary people
   b. are the same as ordinary people
   c. are a lot less happy than ordinary people

5. Experts agree: ____ .
   a. money can't buy happiness
   b. money can make people happier
   c. money can make people a lot less happy

B. Discuss these questions with your classmates.

1. Think about your childhood and today. Are people today happier or less happy? In what ways are you happier today?

2. Is money important for happiness? Why or why not?

7 WORK WITH THE VOCABULARY

A. Read the clues. Complete the crossword puzzle with the words from the box.

| compare | expert | happiness | machine | research | wealthy |

Clues

1. A dishwasher cleans dishes; a washing ____ cleans clothes.

2. We can ____ two times, two places, or two people.

3. Experts do ____ to find information.

4. ____ is a good feeling.

5. Another word for rich is ____.

6. For answers, talk to an ____.

```
     1      2
     M  A   C  H  I  N  E
                          3
                          
  4
                          
                  5
  6
```

B. Read the information in the box.

Comparing with Adjectives

Adjectives describe people, places, and things—*a **happy** person, a **new** place, a **hard** thing*. You can use *a little* and *a lot* to compare adjectives:

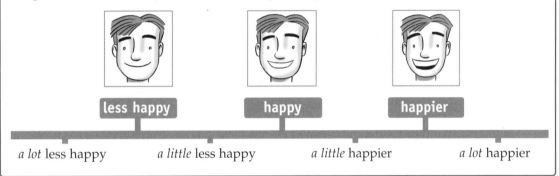

| less happy | happy | happier |

a lot less happy   *a little* less happy   *a little* happier   *a lot* happier

---

C. Look at the chart. Put an X in the correct column. Discuss your answers with a partner.

How happy will this make you?	a lot less happy	a little less happy	a little happier	a lot happier
1. a different job				
2. moving to a new city				
3. an evening out				
4. an email from a friend				
5. a free afternoon				

A. Match the adjective to the people.

1. attractive ___   2. healthy ___   3. intelligent ___

4. lucky ___   5. married ___

B. Take this quiz about happiness. Circle True or False. Then compare your answers with a partner.

HAPPINESS QUIZ: Who is Happier?

1. Young people are happier.	True	False
2. Intelligent people are happier.	True	False
3. Good-looking people are happier.	True	False
4. People with friends are happier.	True	False
5. Married people are happier.	True	False

9 WORDS YOU NEED

Read the definitions. Then match the words and the examples.

advice: a friend's or expert's ideas about the way to do something
positive attitude: a good or happy way of thinking in difficult times
enjoy: to like
get to know: to find out about

_d_ 1. a **positive attitude**
____ 2. things people **enjoy**
____ 3. some **advice**
____ 4. **get to know** someone

a. "I come from a big family. Do you?"
b. "You need to study a lot."
c. "My favorite things are pizza and movies."
d. "I can do it! I can work hard!"

10 USE YOUR READING SKILLS

Preview the article on page 10. Circle your answers.

1. Look at the title. This article is about ____.
   a. new studies
   b. education
   c. happiness

2. Look at the picture and caption. This article has information about ____.
   a. friends and happines
   b. school and happiness
   c. work and happiness

In this magazine article, the writer talks about how to be happy.

What Makes Us HAPPY?

Everyone wants to be happy, but sometimes it isn't easy. What makes people happy? What things aren't important to happiness? Look at this information from some studies[1] by experts.

These things make people happy:
- **Friends.** In a study of college students, all of the very happy students have friends.
- **Positive attitude.** A positive attitude helps people feel happier.
- **Marriage.** In many studies, married people are happier.
- **Good health.** When people feel healthy, they also feel happier.

These things don't make people happy:
- **Money.** Wealthy people are not a lot happier than ordinary people.
- **Age.** Younger and older people are both happy.
- **Intelligence.** Very intelligent people are not always happier.
- **Good looks.** Attractive or beautiful people are not always happier.
- **Luck.** Lucky people aren't always happier than other people. For example, lottery[2] winners are very happy at first, but after five years their lives usually go back to normal. Their happiness is the same as before the lottery.

Friends can make you happy

Do you want to have a happier life? The experts have this advice for you:
1. **Make friends.** Get to know the people at work and in your community.
2. **Spend time with friends and family.** Talk and do fun things with the important people in your life.
3. **Have a positive attitude about your life.** When you see a problem, look for a solution.[3]
4. **Help other people be happy.** People often feel happier when they make someone else happy.

Read the research. Think about the studies. Then follow the experts' advice for a happier life!

[1] **study (*n.*):** a test of or careful look at ideas
[2] **lottery:** a game—many people buy tickets but only one person wins money or a prize
[3] **solution:** a way to fix a problem

12 UNDERSTAND THE READING

A. Read this letter from a student. Think about the advice in the article on page 10. Put an X next to good advice for this student. More than one answer can be correct. Discuss your answers with a partner.

> I'm at a new school, and I don't feel happy. Everything is different. I want to enjoy my school. I want to be happy. Can you give me some advice?

____ 1. Try to make some friends at your new school.
____ 2. Change schools again.
____ 3. Help a student in your class.
____ 4. Don't only think about the problem. Try to find a solution.

B. Look back at the quiz on page 9. Answer the questions again using the information from the article.

C. Think about these questions. Discuss them with your classmates.

The writer's advice is: (1) have a positive attitude, especially about problems, and (2) spend time with friends and family. Is this good advice? Why or why not?

13 WORK WITH THE VOCABULARY

A. Circle the correct word in each sentence.

1. Juan is always happy. He has a very (positive attitude/unhappy attitude) about life.

2. I have an opinion, but my sister has a different opinion. We never (agree/enjoy)!

3. When I have problems, I always talk to my friend. She gives me good (advice/luck).

4. Kimiko likes to make friends. She always (gets to know/compares) friends quickly.

B. Read these sentences from the article on page 10. Look at the underlined phrase. Then choose the word or phrase with the same meaning. Look back at the article for help.

1. When people win the lottery, they are very happy—but soon things are <u>back to normal</u>.
   a. new and more fun   b. the same as before   c. very lucky

2. <u>Spend time with</u> your friends and family—with the important people in your life.
   a. buy gifts for   b. be with   c. think about

GET READY TO READ AND SHARE

Read the notice. Then match the words and the definitions.

HAGERSTOWN COMMUNITY ORGANIZATION

Program for seniors

- Food program; help at home
- Activities (classes, trips . . .)

Program for children

- Help kids with homework
- Activities (sports, games . . .)

Help the People in Your Community—Be a Volunteer!
Can you give a little time to help seniors or kids?

For information,
call 555-5421

_f_ **1.** a program   a. a town or neighborhood
____ **2.** a community   b. a child
____ **3.** a volunteer   c. a helper, working without pay
____ **4.** an activity   d. an old person
____ **5.** a senior   e. something to do
____ **6.** a kid   f. a group of classes or activities

USE YOUR READING SKILLS

A. You are going to read one part of a magazine article. Read the introduction to the article below. Then answer the questions.

Two Volunteers

Each year, about 65 million people in the United States volunteer—about 25% of men and about 32% of women. Who are these people? Why do they volunteer? In this article, we look at two very special women: Delores "Hap" Johnson and Tianna Bailey. Both women are volunteers. Each woman makes a difference in her community.

1. What is this article about? _____

2. How many people in the U.S. are volunteers? _____

B. Preview Part A and Part B of the magazine article below and on page 14. Then answer these questions.

1. Who does Hap Johnson help?   a. seniors   b. children
2. Who does Tianna Bailey help?   a. seniors   b. children

Now choose one part of the article to read. Read Part A on page 13 *or* Part B on page 14.

16 READ PART A

Senior Helps Seniors

Delores "Hap" Johnson is a volunteer for DARTS (Dakota Area Resources and Transportation for Seniors). DARTS, a community program in Minneapolis/St. Paul, Minnesota, helps seniors and their families.

Sometimes it's difficult for seniors to get around town. DARTS buses take them to their medical appointments and the supermarket. Hap goes on the bus with the seniors to help them feel comfortable. When they get off the bus, she helps them with their shopping or spends time with them at the doctor's office.

When Hap isn't on the bus, she's probably walking. She loves to walk. Now in her 70s, Hap walks about 12 miles a week. She also volunteers with the seniors in her apartment building. She plans activities for them and walks with them every day.

"Walking helps seniors stay active[1] and healthy," Hap says. "It helps me stay active, too!" She feels the same way about volunteering. When she volunteers, Hap Johnson is happy because she is helping other people. And that's not all. "I put smiles on their faces," Hap says.

[1]**active:** doing things

Who can answer these questions about Part A with you? Find a partner. Answer the questions.

Focus Questions
1. Who does DARTS help?
2. What does Hap Johnson do for DARTS?
3. Why does she volunteer?

Tianna Bailey Helps Kids

Tianna Bailey is a college student in her 20s. She wants to be a teacher and studies hard at Emory University in Atlanta, Georgia. She is also a volunteer. Tianna works with her cousin, Maurice Shaffer, to help the children in their community. Their program is called IMAGE (**I M**ust **A**chieve the **G**oal to **E**xcel).

IMAGE helps children in the Edgewood Court Apartments in Atlanta. The families in Edgewood Court don't have a lot of money, but IMAGE is free. The children need activities after school and in the summer. IMAGE gives them activities.

IMAGE has an activity room with many games and books. The children enjoy playing there, but first they have to do their homework. Tianna and Maurice tutor[1] the children with help

from other college student volunteers.

Why is Tianna doing all this work? "We want to help kids in our community," Tianna says, "because other people help us."

Volunteering also makes her feel good. "The kids are happier, and they're doing better in school. For me, this is a dream come true.[2]"

[1]**tutor:** to give help with school work
[2]**a dream come true:** a great, special thing

Who can answer these questions about Part B with you? Find a partner. Answer the questions.

Focus Questions

1. Who does IMAGE help?

2. What does Tianna Bailey do for IMAGE?

3. Why does she volunteer?

Organize Your Thoughts

With your partner, mark the information from your part of the article with an X.
Then use that information to complete the questionnaire below.

INFORMATION		
____ She's in her 70s.	____ It helps seniors and their families.	____ She helps kids with their homework.
____ It helps kids in the Edgewood Court Apartments.	____ Hap Johnson	____ DARTS
____ She goes with seniors on buses.	____ The kids are doing better in school!	____ She's in her 20s.
____ Tianna Bailey	____ She can help other people and be active.	____ IMAGE

QUESTIONNAIRE

1. What is the volunteer's name? _____

2. How old is she? _____

3. What is the name of her community program? _____

4. Who does this program help? _____

5. How does she help? _____

6. Why does volunteering make her happy? _____

Share Your Information

Who can tell you about the other part of the article? With your partner, find another
pair of classmates.

1. Share your answers to the questionnaire above with the other pair of students.

2. Add other information from your part of the article.

Share Your Ideas

Discuss these questions with your partner and the other pair of students. Then share
your answers with the class.

1. Why do people volunteer?

2. Do you know any volunteers? What do they do?

3. Volunteering can make people happy. What other
   activities can make people happy?

18 REFLECT ON: Happiness

A. Read these questions. Then read one student's paragraph.

   1. What do you feel happy about? Why?

   2. What do you feel unhappy about? Why? How can you feel happy again?

   3. In your opinion, what is important for happiness?

> I feel happy about new friends. I enjoy our activities. For example, it's fun to play soccer together in the park on Sundays. I feel unhappy about the food in the school cafeteria. It is usually bad. How can I feel happy again? I can learn to cook and make my own food. In my opinion, small things like good food are very important for happiness.

B. In a small group, discuss these questions.

   1. What is this student unhappy about? Why? What is his solution?

   2. Do you agree with the student's idea about happiness? Why or why not?

C. Now write your own paragraph. First, write your answers to the questions in A. Then add some examples. You can use the student's paragraph as a model.

It's Great to Communicate!

In this unit, you are going to:
- read about communicating in the U.S.
- learn how to preview and predict

WHAT DO YOU KNOW ABOUT COMMUNICATION?

A. Look at the pictures from one student's day. Who is he communicating with?
   Why is he communicating? Discuss your answers with your classmates.

B. Think about a usual day in your life. Who do you communicate with? Why?
   In your notebook, list three different communication experiences from your
   usual day. Follow the example below. Share your chart with a partner.

When?	With Whom?	Why?
7:30, at home	my roommate	to say good morning
9:00, at school	my English teacher and classmates	to answer questions, to discuss with the class
12:30, on e-mail	my cousin in Japan	to chat about school and family

A. When were you born? Put your name in the correct column of the chart below. Add the names of your family, friends, and other people in your life.

Before 1945	1946–1964	1965–1980	1981–now

B. With your classmates, discuss the differences between the groups of people—the *generations* of people—in your chart.

C. When people of different generations don't understand each other, we call it a generation gap. Read these statements. Mark examples of a generation gap with an X. Check your answers with a partner.

____ a. "The young people in this office don't want to work hard. Our generation has a better attitude about work."

____ b. "My friends change plans too often. I don't like to change plans."

____ c. "In my opinion, 12:00 at night is early. In my parents' opinion, it's late."

____ d. "My children and I listen to the same music!"

2 **BUILD YOUR READING SKILLS: Previewing and Predicting**

Introduction

With a partner, look at the article and answer the questions.

1. Maya wants to learn how to communicate better with her parents. Can this article perhaps help her?

TALKING WITH SENIORS

xxxxxxxxxxxxxxxxxxxxxxxxxxxxxx
xxxxxxxxxxxxxxxxxxxxxxxxxxxxxx
xxxxxxxxxxxxxxxxxxxxxxxxxxxx
xxxxxxxxxxxxxxxxxxxxxxxxxxxxx

Spend time together

---

2. What information might be in this article? Why do you think so?

Reading Skill

Previewing and predicting help you understand a text. After you preview, ask yourself a prediction question: *What will I learn in this article?* When you read the text, check your prediction.

Preview This		To Predict This
title	⟶	What is the topic of this article?
pictures, charts, captions, and any introduction to the text	⟶	What will I learn about in this article?

Practice Previewing and Making Predictions

With a partner, preview the text and make predictions. Answer the questions.

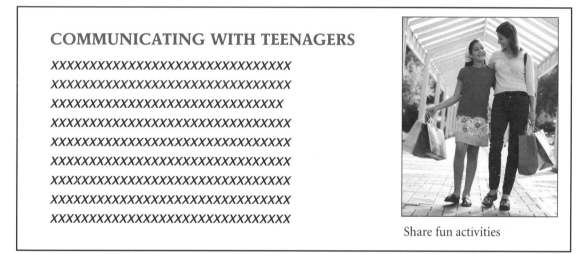

COMMUNICATING WITH TEENAGERS

XXXXXXXXXXXXXXXXXXXXXXXXXXXXXX
XXXXXXXXXXXXXXXXXXXXXXXXXXXXXX
XXXXXXXXXXXXXXXXXXXXXXXXXXXXX
XXXXXXXXXXXXXXXXXXXXXXXXXXXXXX
XXXXXXXXXXXXXXXXXXXXXXXXXXXXXX
XXXXXXXXXXXXXXXXXXXXXXXXXXXXXX
XXXXXXXXXXXXXXXXXXXXXXXXXXXXX
XXXXXXXXXXXXXXXXXXXXXXXXXXXXX
XXXXXXXXXXXXXXXXXXXXXXXXXXXXXX

Share fun activities

1. What is the topic of the article? Circle your answer.

    a. how parents can communicate with teenagers
    b. how teenagers can communicate with parents

2. What can you predict about the article? Mark your predictions with an X.

    ___a. advice about shopping for teenagers

    ___b. advice about communicating with teenagers

    ___c. advice about good activities for parents and teenagers

    ___d. advice about teenage health problems

3 WORDS YOU NEED

Match the parents' statements to the actions. Guess the answers. Then discuss your answers with your classmates.

Action	Parent's statements to their teenagers
_e_ **1.** discuss problems	a. "Be home by 8:00 on school nights and 11:00 on weekends."
___ **2.** make rules	b. "No. We're not buying a second car."
___ **3.** express feelings	c. "Do you like your classes? Tell me about them."
___ **4.** make decisions	d. "You kids make me happy!"
___ **5.** show interest	e. "Your grades aren't good. We need to talk."

4 USE YOUR READING SKILLS

A. Preview the text on page 21. Mark the topic of the text with an X.

_____ **a.** the generation gap in the U.S.

_____ **b.** the number of people in the U.S.

_____ **c.** one American family

B. What will the article discuss? Mark your predictions with an X. As you read the article, check your predictions.

_____ **a.** the generation gap in the U.S.

_____ **b.** family life in the U.S.

_____ **c.** generation gaps in other countries

_____ **d.** types of communication

_____ **e.** communication and generation gaps

In some families, there is a generation gap between parents and teenagers. This magazine article discusses that gap and tells about a new style of communication.

FAMILY COMMUNICATION
Making the Generation Gap Smaller

P eople from different generations often live and work together. Sometimes they're happy being together, other times they're not. One of the reasons for their unhappiness may be a generation gap. A generation gap is the difference between two or more generations—not the differences between their years but the differences between the generations' ideas, attitudes, and interests.[1] Of course, people can have differences and still be happy together, but according to the experts, communication between the generations helps everyone get along.[2]

Good communication between the generations starts in the family. These days many families are changing their communication style.[3] They are moving from a "one-way" style to a "two-way" style of communication. To show this change, let's compare two families:

One-way communication

- The Smith family uses the "one-way" style of communication. Mr. and Mrs. Smith show interest in their children, but they don't discuss problems or feelings. The parents make all the rules and decisions. They don't ask for their children's opinions. They explain their decisions to their children, but they don't discuss them. The explanation is clear and the children understand. The communication goes one way: from the parents to the children.

Two-way communication

- The Jones family uses the "two-way" style of communication. Mr. and Mrs. Jones show interest in their children and ask for their opinions. They discuss problems and express their feelings. The family makes rules and decisions together after a discussion. The communication goes two ways: from parents to children and from children to parents.

Better communication between generations at home means better communication between generations at work and in the community. When different generations learn about each other's ideas, attitudes, and interests, they understand each other. This understanding makes relationships[4] stronger and makes the generation gap smaller.

[1] **interests:** things a person likes to do or to learn about
[2] **get along:** be happy together
[3] **style:** way of doing something
[4] **relationship:** the connection between people

6 UNDERSTAND THE READING

A. Circle the correct answer.

1. Is the generation gap in the U.S. getting bigger or smaller?

    a. bigger
    b. smaller
    c. Experts don't agree.

2. What is the reason for the change in the generation gap?

    a. good families
    b. good generation gaps
    c. good communication

3. Where does good communication begin?

    a. in the world
    b. in families
    c. in everyday life

4. Which style of communication helps make the generation gap smaller?

    a. the one-way style
    b. the two-way style
    c. both styles

5. Where can generation gaps happen?

    a. only in families
    b. only in families and at work
    c. in all parts of life

B. Work in a small group. Discuss the questions. Then discuss your answers with your classmates.

1. In your experience, how big is the generation gap today? Mark your answer on the scale. Give some examples to support your answer.

very small	small	not big, not small	very big	big

2. Which communication style is better for families: one-way or two-way? Why?

A. Complete the sentences with a phrase from the box. Use each phrase one time.

discuss problems	express feelings	make decisions
make rules	show interest	

1. Most parents _____ _____ in their children. They want to know about their children's lives and ideas.

2. In some families, only the parents _____ _____ and _____ _____. The parents explain them to the children, but they do not want their children's opinions.

3. Communication in the family is very important. Parents and children need to _____ _____ and find solutions together.

4. Sometimes, a teenager is unhappy, but the parents don't know it. Children need to be able to _____ _____ to their parents openly

Suffixes: -tion/-sion

You can use the suffix -tion or -sion to form nouns from some verbs. For example,

communicate + -tion = communication

(The -e at the end of some verbs disappears.)

B. Use -tion or -sion to form nouns from the verbs below. Look back at the article on page 21 to find the right form. The paragraph numbers can help you find the nouns.

Verb	Noun	Paragraph
a. communicate	communication	1
b. decide		4
c. explain		4
d. discuss		5

A. Look at the pictures and read the captions. What are these people saying and doing? Share your ideas with your classmates.

get angry   interrupt   pay attention

B. Take this quiz about communication. Circle your answers.

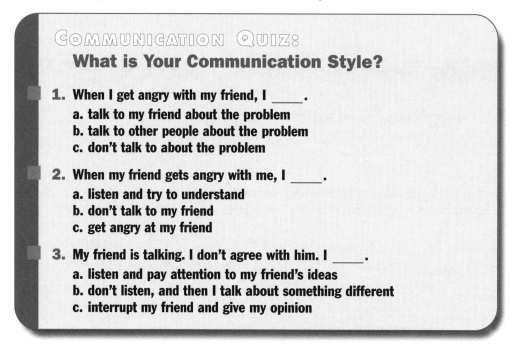

COMMUNICATION QUIZ:

What is Your Communication Style?

1. When I get angry with my friend, I _____.
   a. talk to my friend about the problem
   b. talk to other people about the problem
   c. don't talk to about the problem

2. When my friend gets angry with me, I _____.
   a. listen and try to understand
   b. don't talk to my friend
   c. get angry at my friend

3. My friend is talking. I don't agree with him. I _____.
   a. listen and pay attention to my friend's ideas
   b. don't listen, and then I talk about something different
   c. interrupt my friend and give my opinion

C. Discuss the quiz and your answers with your classmates.

9 WORDS YOU NEED

Read the words and their definitions. Then use one of them to complete the statements about each communication problem.

> **avoid:** to stop something from happening
> **(be) honest:** to say true things
> **kind:** nice
> **misunderstanding:** a problem in communication
> **solve:** to find a solution

1. Jana asked Camilla, "Do you like my new sweater?" Camilla said, "No, it's ugly." Then Jana got angry with Camilla.

   Camilla thinks, "I am _____," but she isn't being _____ to Jana.

2. Tomas and Maria are having a discussion. Tomas doesn't understand Maria's opinion, and Maria doesn't understand Tomas's opinion.

   There is a _____ in Tomas and Maria's communication.

3. " I have a problem, but I don't want to discuss things with my family," said Marco. "Maybe they will get angry at me."

   Marco is trying to _____ a discussion, but he can't. He needs to tell his family about his problem. They can try to _____ it together.

10 USE YOUR READING SKILLS

Preview the article on page 26 and make predictions. Answer the questions.

1. What is the topic of the article? Circle your answer.

   a. communication can help you make friends
   b. communication can help you have an argument
   c. communication can help you solve problems

2. What will the article discuss? Mark your predictions with an X. As you read the article, check your predictions.

   ____a. rules for communicating with teenagers

   ____b. rules for communicating with friends

   ____c. advice about communicating with seniors.

   ____d. advice about good activities to do with friends.

   ____e. advice about how to solve problems.

This magazine article gives readers some simple rules to follow to help them communicate better.

6 COMMUNICATION RULES FOR FRIENDS AND FAMILY

Communication is a very important part of life. We want to get along with friends and family, and these six simple rules can help.

> **Rule #1: Talk it out!**
> **Rule #2: Be honest, but also be kind**
> **Rule #3: Be clear**
> **Rule #4: Don't interrupt**
> **Rule #5: Try to understand other ideas**
> **Rule #6: Think about solutions**

■ *Talk it out!* When you have a problem with a friend, it's good to express your feelings. You can avoid large problems when you talk out small problems. The first rule of communication is . . . communicate!

■ *Be honest, but also be kind.* Angry people sometimes want to say something bad or mean. This is dangerous. Words can hurt people, and they can hurt a relationship forever.[1] When you get angry, think before you speak. And remember, sometimes the best idea is to say nothing—to keep quiet.

■ *Be clear.* It is important to explain your ideas clearly. When you don't understand your friend's ideas, ask for an explanation. This will help you avoid misunderstandings.

■ *Don't interrupt.* We all like to talk, but listening is important, too. When you and a friend have a problem, listen to your friend. Pay attention and don't interrupt!

■ *Try to understand other ideas.* Problems sometimes happen when two people have different ideas or opinions. One person's ideas are never all right, and the other person's ideas are never all wrong. Probably, some ideas from both people are right. Right or wrong, all of the ideas are important. Think about your friend's ideas and try to understand them.

■ *Think about solutions, not problems.* When it is hard to see the solution to a problem, people sometimes only think about the problem. Try not to think about the problem. Think about solutions! Ask yourself, What can we do to solve the problem?

No one wants to have misunderstandings. These six simple rules really can help you solve your communication problems. Can you remember the rules? No problem!

[1] **forever:** always, without an end

12 UNDERSTAND THE READING

A. These people have communication problems. Which rule from the article can help them? Match the best rule to the problem. Compare your answers with a partner.

PROBLEM

_____ **1. Laura:** I'm angry at my daughter. She uses my things all the time.
Marta: What does she say when you tell her this?
Laura: I can't tell her!

_____ **2. Liu:** Look! I just bought a car! I'm so happy! Do you like it?
Max: No, not really. It's very old and ugly.

_____ **3. Tibor:** Are you ready to go?
Benny: Sorry, no, I just have to . . .
Tibor: We planned to leave at 2! You know that! I'm not going to wait for you.

_____ **4. Delores:** I want to visit my family this weekend, but I don't have a car. I can go this weekend, but I don't have a car. I *want* to go, but I can't go because I don't have a car.

RULE

a. Talk it out

b. Be honest, but also be kind

c. Be clear

d. Don't interrupt

e. Be open to other ideas

f. Think about solutions

B. Look back at the quiz on page 24. Answer the questions again using the information from the article.

C. Work with a partner. Discuss these questions. Then share your answers with your classmates.

1. Which rule of communication is the most important? Why?

2. Which rule is the most difficult for people to follow? Why?

3. Which rule is the most difficult for you to follow? Why?

13 WORK WITH THE VOCABULARY

Read the sentences. Look at the underlined words. Then circle the word(s) with the *opposite* meaning.

1. Let him finish talking. Don't (interrupt / get angry at) him.

2. He's a very nice person. He never says (unkind / important) things.

3. I try to be honest and clear. I want to avoid (misunderstandings / rules).

4. Don't let problems happen. Try to (avoid / understand) problems.

14 GET READY TO READ AND SHARE

Read the message board. Then complete the paragraph below with the underlined words in the message board.

File   Edit   View   Tools   Help

◀ Back   ▶ Forward   ⊗ Stop   ⇆ Refresh   🏠 Home

GOOD COMMUNICATION MESSAGE BOARD

Do you have a communication problem or question? Follow these steps to get advice from people around the world!

1. Write about your problem in a <u>message</u>.
2. Put, or <u>post</u>, your message. Everyone can read it.
3. Wait for a <u>reply</u> from someone.
4. Post your own reply back.

Remember our rules: Don't use your real name—use a <u>screen name</u>. Also, put the topic of your message in the <u>Subject</u> line of the message.

   Message boards are Internet Web sites for people to share ideas. People write their ideas or ask questions in a _____ . Then they put it on the site,
   1

or _____ it. The _____ line gives the topic. Other
   2   3

people read it and send an answer, or _____ . Most people don't use
   4

their real name on a message board. They use a _____ .
   5

---

15 USE YOUR READING SKILLS

A. You are going to read an Internet message and a reply. Read the message below. Then answer the questions on the next page.

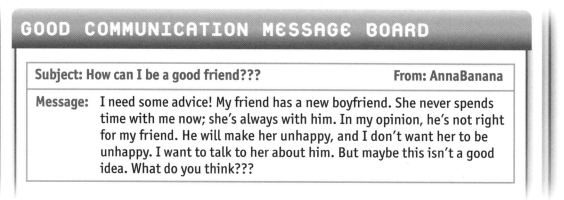

GOOD COMMUNICATION MESSAGE BOARD

Subject: How can I be a good friend???	From: AnnaBanana

Message: I need some advice! My friend has a new boyfriend. She never spends time with me now; she's always with him. In my opinion, he's not right for my friend. He will make her unhappy, and I don't want her to be unhappy. I want to talk to her about him. But maybe this isn't a good idea. What do you think???

1. Why doesn't AnnaBanana's friend spend time with her now?

2. What is AnnaBanana's opinion of the boyfriend?

B. Preview the replies to AnnaBanana's message below and on page 30. Look at their Subject lines. Then predict the answers to these questions.

1. What is Sunshine's advice?

    a. Talk to her.   b. Don't talk to her.

2. What is Cowgirl's advice?

    a. Talk to her.   b. Don't talk to her.

Now choose one reply to read. Read Reply A below _or_ Reply B on page 30.

16 READ REPLY A

GOOD COMMUNICATION MESSAGE BOARD

Subject: Keep quiet!!	From: Sunshine

Message:	Hi AnnaBanana, You want your friend to be happy. So don't talk to her. Think about this: You say something. Then what happens? She feels hurt or angry—and unhappy. And that's the end of your friendship.[1] Remember, friends don't always agree. You and your friend are different people. Maybe her boyfriend is not right for you, but maybe he is right for her! Also, you usually spend lots of time with your friend, but now you don't see her often. Maybe you are a little jealous.[2] So this is my advice: keep quiet, and try to understand her feelings.

[1] **friendship:** the relationship between friends
[2] **jealous:** feeling sad or angry because you want something another person has

Who can answer these questions about Reply A with you? Find a partner. Answer the questions.

Focus Questions

1. Why shouldn't AnnaBanana talk to her friend?

2. In Sunshine's opinion, why is AnnaBanana jealous?

GOOD COMMUNICATION MESSAGE BOARD

RE: Subject: Keep quiet!!	From: Sunshine

Subject: You have to say something!	From: Cowgirl

Message:	AnnaBanana,

You want your friend to be happy. So talk to her! Discuss your feelings and her feelings. It helps to listen to other people's ideas. Other people's ideas can help you think better. So help your friend: Tell her your ideas. Give your friend advice before she makes a bad decision. Don't wait for her to be unhappy!

Remember, friends don't always agree. You need to talk it out. You can keep quiet and avoid an argument,[1] but you're not being honest. And soon your friendship[2] will feel false, not real.

Your idea is a good idea. Talk to your friend!

[1]**argument:** an angry discussion
[2]**friendship:** the relationship between friends

Who can answer these questions about Reply B with you? Find a partner. Answer the questions.

Focus Questions

1. Why do we need other people's ideas?

2. In Cowgirl's opinion, it's bad to avoid a problem with a friend? Why?

Organize Your Thoughts

Work with your partner. Read the sentences. Which sentences have ideas from your reply? Mark them with an X. Then copy those sentences into the area for your reply below.

Sentences

____ Talk to her.

____ Don't talk to her.

____ You want your friend to be happy.

____ Your ideas can help her think better.

____ Friends don't always agree.

____ You need to be honest with her.

____ Maybe her boyfriend is right for her.

____ Maybe you are jealous.

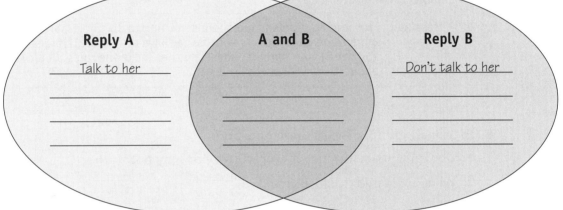

Share Your Information

Who can tell you about the other reply? Find a pair of classmates.

1. With your partner, tell the other pair of students about your reply. Use your sentences from the chart above, and add other information from your reply.

2. Compare charts with the other pair of students. Some of the sentences are in both replies. Write these sentences in the middle section, marked "A and B."

Share Your Ideas

Discuss these questions with your partner and the other pair of students. Then share your advice with the class.

1. Which message has better advice? Why?

2. What is your advice to AnnaBanana?

A. Read this message. Then read one student's reply.

Back   Forward   Stop   Refresh   Home

Subject: What can I do???	**From: Techie**

Message: I'm 20 years old. I work and go to college, but I live with my parents. My dad is the problem. I can't do things at night with my friends. They stay out late. My dad wants me to be home by 11:00! That's early! What should I do? He doesn't want to hear my ideas.

RE: Subject: Generation Gap	**From: ChelsB**

Message: This is a big problem, but there's nothing to do. The problem is the generation gap. You and your father have different attitudes and ideas. You live in your parents' house, so they make the rules. Don't try to talk about it. Just follow the rules.

B. In a small group, discuss these questions.

1. Do you agree with ChelsB's reply? Why or why not?

2. What is your advice to Techie?

C. Now write a reply to Techie and give your advice. Answer the questions and add some details. You can use the reply above as a model.

1. Is Techie's problem big or small?

2. What should Techie do? Why?

Post a Reply

Message:

Unit 3

Success in the U.S.

In this unit, you are going to:

- read about different kinds of success in the U.S.
- learn how to connect pronouns to nouns

WHAT IS SUCCESS?

A. Look at this picture. This woman is celebrating her success. What did she do? Why does she feel successful? Discuss your answers with your classmates.

B. Think about these statements. Do you agree or disagree with them? Why? Discuss your opinions with your classmates.

1. There are many different kinds of success.

2. Hard work is usually necessary for success.

3. People must have money to succeed.

A. Look at these pictures from the covers of two books. Then answer the questions below. Discuss your answers with your classmates.

1. When do these stories happen—now or in the past? How do you know?

2. How old are the boys in the pictures? Are they rich or poor? How do they make money?

3. What can you predict about these stories? What might happen to the boys?

B. Work with a partner. Look at the adjectives in the box. Which ones do you know? Ask classmates about any new words, or look them up in a dictionary.

dishonest	hard-working	honest	kind	lazy	polite

C. Put each adjective from the box above into the correct column of the chart. Then add one word to each column.

positive	negative
polite	

BUILD YOUR READING SKILLS: Connecting Pronouns to Nouns

Introduction

A. Look at the picture. What is the speaker talking about?

Then she told them to finish it by tomorrow.

B. Can you answer the question in A? What information do you need?

Reading Skill

A pronoun takes the place of a noun. **Connecting every pronoun to a noun** tells you the meaning of the pronoun.

Example

Horatio Alger is the writer of *Ragged Dick*. **It** is **his** eighth book.
(Usually, the noun comes before its pronoun.)

Practice Connecting Pronouns to Nouns

Look at the pronouns in bold. What noun does each pronoun connect to? Underline the noun, and draw a line from the pronoun to the noun.

Dick was a shoeshine boy. **He** started work early. People hurried

down the street. Dick called to **them**, "Shoeshine?" No one stopped, but

Dick didn't worry. **He** had a positive attitude.

Soon Mr. Greyson walked by. He saw Dick. Mr. Greyson looked

down at **his** shoes. **They** looked dirty. He walked over to Dick. And

Dick had his first job of the day!

3 WORDS YOU NEED

Read the sentences. Guess the meaning of the underlined word. Match each one to a definition. Check your guesses after you read the article on page 37.

____ 1. That novel has a very interesting hero.

____ 2. Our friends can influence us in good and bad ways.

____ 3. My grades aren't very good; I need to improve them.

____ 4. This year wasn't a good year, but I have more hope for next year.

a. to make something better

b. to change someone/something in some way

c. good feelings about the future

d. the most important person in a book

4 USE YOUR READING SKILLS

Preview the article on page 37 and make predictions. Answer the questions.

1. What is the topic of the article? Circle your answer.

   a. the life of Horatio Alger and other writers
   b. many people's ideas about success in the U.S.
   c. Horatio Alger changed ideas about success in the U.S.

2. What will the article discuss? Mark your predictions with an X. As you read the article, check your predictions.

   ____ a. Horatio Alger's work as a writer

   ____ b. life in an earlier time in the U.S.

   ____ c. how Alger's stories changed ideas of success

   ____ d. the people in Horatio Alger's stories

   ____ e. writers in U.S. history

Horatio Alger was an important writer in U.S. history. This Web page gives information about him and his stories.

File   Edit   View   Tools   Help

Back   Forward   Stop   Refresh   Home

Horatio Alger

HOW HE INFLUENCED THE IDEA OF SUCCESS IN THE UNITED STATES

Horatio Alger was one of the most successful writers in United States history. In the early 1900s, his books were in almost every home and influenced several generations of boys. Alger wrote[1] more than 400 novels and more than 500 short stories. How was this possible for one man? He always wrote the same story! In a Horatio Alger story, the details[2] change, but the story and the hero stay the same.

In a typical Horatio Alger story, the hero—a poor teenage boy—finds success. The boy has no parents or family. He did not go to school, but he is smart and wants to learn. He is hardworking, honest, and kind. He always helps other people. The hero has a positive attitude and believes in himself. He wants to succeed, and he is not afraid[3] to try new things.

The hero goes to a city. He works very hard and makes a little money. He tries to improve his life. For example, he learns to read. Later, he meets a rich man, and this man helps him. Then he has some good luck.

With this luck, his hard work, and the rich man, the hero gets a good job and becomes successful.

Horatio Alger's stories were popular because they were similar to real life for many people. In the early 1900s, immigrants and many other people went[4] to cities for jobs. These cities were big and dirty, and life was hard. Many families were very poor. Often, even young children worked. Like the boys in the stories, these people also wanted to find success. Alger wanted to give them hope with this message: In the United States, poor people can succeed.

Horatio Alger's message is still a main idea of U.S. culture today. It is now part of the culture and the language. When you hear people talking about a poor person's success, listen! Someone will probably say, "That is a real Horatio Alger story!"

[1] **wrote:** past tense of *write*
[2] **detail:** small piece of information
[3] **be afraid:** to fear something
[4] **went:** past tense of *go*

A. Read the sentences. Are they true or false? Put an X under True or False for each sentence.

Sentence	True	False
1. Horatio Alger wrote many novels and many short stories.		
2. Horatio Alger often wrote about teenage girls.		
3. Horatio Alger wanted his books to give people hope.		
4. Horatio Alger influenced the American idea of success.		
5. Horatio Alger's books were in few homes in the U.S.		

B. Read these sentences from a story. Which of them can you find in a typical Horatio Alger story? Mark your answers with an X. Compare your answers with a partner.

____1. George lived in a city.

____2. George lived with his family.

____3. George was poor.

____4. George was lazy.

____5. George had a negative attitude.

____6. George learned to read.

____7. George helped a little boy.

C. Work in a small group. Discuss these questions.

1. Horatio Alger's books influenced many people. What books, people, or things influence you?

2. Horatio Alger's stories express this idea: In the U.S., hardworking people can find a good job and live a good life. Do you agree? Why or why not?

7 WORK WITH THE VOCABULARY

A. Complete the story with the words from the box. Use each word one time.

| a. hero | b. hope | c. improve | d. influenced |

Tom was a very lazy boy. He stayed in bed most of the time. He was afraid to try new things. His parents did not have much _____ for him and his
1
future. "He cannot succeed. He has a negative attitude," they said.

One day, Tom read some Horatio Alger stories, and they really _____
2
him. He decided to change his life. "I can _____ in so many ways," Tom
3
said. "I can be more hardworking, like the _____ in the story!" Tom and his
4
parents were happy.

B. Look at the words in the chart and notice their forms. Use the chart to help you complete the sentences below with the correct form.

noun	verb	adjective
success	succeed	successful

1. Horatio Alger was one of the most _____ writers in U.S. history.

2. In a typical Horatio Alger story, a poor teenage boy finds _____.

3. He wants to _____ and he isn't afraid to try new things.

4. The hero gets a good job and becomes _____.

5. This is Alger's message: In the United States, poor people can _____.

6. A "real Horatio Alger story" is a story about a poor person's _____.

8 GET READY TO READ ABOUT: Finding the Right Job

A. Look at the cartoon. Discuss the questions below with your classmates.

1. What is the situation? Who are these two men?

2. What does "dress for success" mean?

3. Is the young man successful? Does he like his job? Why or why not?

B. Complete the questionnaire. Write many answers for each question. Then discuss your answers with a partner.

What kind of job is right for you?
1. What do you like to do? What are your interests?
2. What do you do well? What are your skills?
3. What jobs match these interests and skills?

C. Work in small groups. Think of three different jobs. For each job, answer these questions. Share your answers with your classmates.

1. What interests go well with this job?

2. What skills do you need for this job?

9 WORDS YOU NEED

Look at the pictures. Match the sentences to the pictures.

1.____

2.____

3.____

4.____

5.____

6.____

a. Jon has an interview at the Ace Supply Company.
b. Jon looks at Help Wanted ads.
c. The Ace Supply Company hires Jon.
d. Jon thinks about his skills.
e. Now Jon is an employee of the Ace Supply Company.
f. Jon writes his resume.

10 USE YOUR READING SKILLS

Preview the article on page 42 and make predictions. Answer the questions.

Preview the article on page 42

1. What is the topic of the article?

    a. advice about living in the U.S.
    b. advice about work in the U.S.
    c. advice about finding a job in the U.S.

2. **What will this article discuss? Mark your predictions with an X. As you read the article, check your predictions.**

    ____a. how to find the right job

    ____b. what to wear on your first day

    ____c. where to find job ads

    ____d. when to stop looking for a job

    ____e. who to ask for advice about jobs

Success often begins with a good job. How can people today find a good job? In this student magazine, an expert on jobs gives some advice.

Business

How to Find the Right Job and *Get It!*

Ana Gomez is a job counselor at Piedmont Bay Community College. She helps students find a job when they finish school. Mark Blain interviewed Ana and asked her to share advice with us.

Question: Ana, you see a lot of students. What's your most important advice for them, and our readers?

Answer: That's easy, Mark. Look for the right job for you. You spend so much time at work. It's very important to like your work and your workplace.

Q What should people think about when they are looking for a job?

A Think about these two questions: What are your interests? What are your skills? Really think about them and write down everything. Then think about this question: What kinds of jobs match your interests and skills? You might need to do some research. Go to the library and read about jobs. Also talk to people in different jobs. Ask them about their work activities. Maybe they can give you ideas for yourself.

Q Where should people look for jobs? In newspaper ads?

A Yes, but also on Internet job sites and on a company's own web site. When you send your resume, it should be clear and neat. It should include your work experience, education, and skills.

Q Okay, so the company called and wants to interview me. What is your advice for the interview?

A Be prepared! Ask yourself, Why should this employer[1] hire me? Think of some good reasons and match them to your skills and experience. And remember, an employer wants employees to be on time and look neat. So be on time for the interview and look neat. Ask questions to show your interest in the job and in the company. Be polite. And stay relaxed![2] Follow this advice and you have a good chance of finding, and getting, the right job for you.

[1] **employer:** an employee's boss
[2] **relaxed:** calm, not worried

12 UNDERSTAND THE READING

A. Complete the sentences. Circle the correct word or phrase.

1. This article is an interview with Ana Gomez, <u>an employer / a job counselor</u>.

2. Ana's most important advice is: <u>Find the right job. / Write a clear resume.</u>

3. In Ana's opinion, you <u>should / shouldn't</u> look at job ads in the newspaper.

4. At the interview, you <u>should / shouldn't</u> ask the employer questions.

B. Draw a line from each pronoun in bold to its noun.

1. Mark Blain interviewed Ana and asked **her** to share advice with us.

2. You can find job ads in the Help Wanted section of the newspaper. You can also find **them** on Internet job sites.

3. Your resume should be clear and neat. **It** should include your experience education, and skills.

4. Employers want their employees to be on time. **They** also want **them** to look neat.

13 WORK WITH THE VOCABULARY

Work with a partner. For each item, write a sentence using all the words. Share your sentences with the class.

1. experience   resume

   Include all your **experience** on your **resume**.

2. employer   company

   _____

3. research   library

   _____

4. job   newspaper ads

   _____

5. interview   on time

   _____

A. With your partner, decide on an order for the pictures. Then tell a story about the pictures. Use the time expressions *First, Then,* and *Finally.* Add your own details.

Example: Phillip wanted to be a lawyer. First, he ...

15 USE YOUR READING SKILLS

A. You are going to read a true story from a book about immigrants. Read the introduction to the book below. Then answer the questions.

Introduction

The United States is a country of immigrants—immigrants from all over the world. Every year, millions of people come to the United States with the dream to build new lives.

This book is about immigrants today. It is about their lives, their dreams, and their success stories—large and small.

1. How many immigrants come to the U.S. every year?

2. What is this book about?

B. Preview Story A and Story B on pages 45 and 46. Then answer the questions.

1. What was Napoleon Barragan's dream?   a. a business   b. a home

2. What was Dorothea Sandiford's dream?   a. a business   b. a home

Now choose one story to read. Read Story A on page 45 *or* Story B on page 46.

Napoleon Barragan: A New Kind of Business

Napoleon Barragan was born in Ecuador. He moved to the United States in 1969. His first jobs in the United States were in factories.[1] He and his wife worked very hard and saved their money. Then, in 1975, they opened their own furniture store.

One day, Napoleon Barragan had an idea. People always went to a store to buy a mattress[2] for their bed. Then they waited for the store to deliver the mattress. There was no other way. Napoleon Barragan decided to give people an easier way to get a new mattress. In 1976, he started a new kind of company. People called the company, at any time of the day or night, and ordered a mattress. Then the company delivered the mattress to their home very quickly.

Napoleon Barragan didn't need a store, so he was able to sell mattresses at a low price. And people always remembered the name of the company and the phone number, because they were the same: 1-800-MATTRESS.

Napoleon Barragan's business did very well. By the year 2000, it was selling millions of mattresses every year. Today, the business is doing even better. And of course, customers can now order their mattress on the Internet.

Napoleon Barragan's dream was to have a successful business. With hard work, the help of his family, and his good idea, he is now living his dream.

[1] **factory:** a place where people make things, usually with machines
[2] **mattress:** the thick, soft part of a bed

Who can answer these questions about Story A with you? Find a partner. Answer the questions.

Focus Questions

1. What was Napoleon Barragan's idea for a company?

2. What are some reasons for his success?

Dorothea Sandiford: A House of Her Own

Dorothea Sandiford was born in Barbados, an island in the Caribbean Sea. She moved to the United States in 1970. When she lived in Barbados, she had a dream. She wanted to have her own house—not an apartment, a house. When she moved to the United States, her dream moved with her.

Dorothea Sandiford needed money to buy a house, but she didn't have much. She didn't even have a job. She decided to make a plan and follow it to her dream.

Dorothea Sandiford worked very hard. She never finished school in Barbados, so she studied for the high school equivalency exam[1] in the United States. She passed it! Then she needed to find a job. She found[2] two! For many years, Dorothea Sandiford worked in a bank during the week and worked as a nurse's aide[3] on the weekends. Every month, she saved a little more money.

Finally, in 1985, Dorothea Sandiford had enough money to buy a house. It was perfect for her. She loved her house and wanted to spend more time there. So, in 1993, she started a day care[4] business in her house.

Today, Dorothea Sandiford still runs her day care business, and she still works on weekends. She also volunteers in her community. She is a very busy woman, but she always finds time to enjoy her home.

Dorothea Sandiford's dream was to have her own house. After years of hard work, she is now living her dream.

[1] **high school equivalency exam (GED):** the test to get a diploma—equal to a high school diploma
[2] **found:** past tense of *find*
[3] **nurse's aide:** a nurse's helper
[4] **day care:** babysitting

Who can answer these questions about Story B with you? Find a partner. Answer the questions.

Focus Questions

1. What was Dorothea Sandiford's dream?

2. What are some reasons for her success?

Organize Your Thoughts

Work with your partner. Find the time line for your story. What happened at each point on the time line? Write your answers. Look back at your story for help.

Napoleon Barragan

*moved to
the U.S.*

1969	1975	1976	2000	Today

Dorothea Sandiford

*moved to
the U.S.*

1970	1985	1993	Today

Share Your Information

Who can tell you about the other story? Find another pair of classmates.

1. With your partner, tell the other pair of students about your story. Use the information from your time line above.

2. Add details from your story.

Share Your Ideas

Discuss this question with your partner and the other pair of students. Then share your answer with the class.

The boys in Horatio Alger's stories succeeded through hard work, a positive attitude, luck, and someone's help. How did Napoleon Barragan and Dorothea Sandiford succeed?

18 REFLECT ON: Success

A. **Read these questions. Then read one student's answers.**

1. Do you know a successful person? Who is this person?

2. How did this person become successful? What did he or she do?

3. Did he or she have any help? What kind of help? Who helped him or her?

4. What is this person doing now?

> My cousin Luis is a successful person now. In elementary school, Luis had very serious problems with reading and writing. His grades were always very bad, and he didn't like school. But Luis always wanted to be a firefighter. Firefighters need to have a high school diploma and go to college. So Luis worked very hard. His teachers, friends, and family helped him. Now he is in college. For us, Luis is a big success.

B. **In a small group, discuss these questions.**

1. In what way is Luis successful?

2. How did he become successful?

3. Did he have any help? Who helped him?

C. **Now write your own paragraph. Answers the questions in A. Then add some details. You can use the student's paragraph as a model.**

Unit 4

Keeping Calm

In this unit, you are going to:
- read about ways people deal with anger in the U.S.
- learn how to understand vocabulary in context

WHAT DO YOU KNOW ABOUT CONTROLLING ANGER?

A. Look at the picture. What is this person feeling? Why? What situations make you feel this way? Discuss your answers with your classmates.

I need some milk for my coffee. Oh, no! My roommate did it again! She drank all the milk!

B. Imagine these situations. Do they make you feel angry? Why or why not? What do you do when you feel angry? Discuss your answers with your classmates.

1. Someone left chewing gum on your bus seat. Now the gum is on your coat!

2. You're driving home from work. The traffic isn't moving. Every day is the same!

3. Your neighbor is having a party. The music is very loud. You have a test tomorrow, but you can't study with all the noise!

1 GET READY TO READ ABOUT: Dealing with Anger

A. Take this quiz. For each sentence, put an X under True or False. Guess the answers.

What do you know about anger?	True	False
1. Anger is a normal feeling.		
2. Most people feel some anger several times a week.		
3. Anger can sometimes help people.		
4. People should always keep their anger inside and should not express it. This is healthy.		
5. People should always express their anger. For example, they should throw things. This is healthy.		
6. Anger can cause health problems.		

B. Work in small groups. Discuss the questions. Then share your answers with your classmates.

1. When you're angry, is your behavior—your words and actions—good or bad?

2. How do you behave when you're angry? What do you do?

2 BUILD YOUR READING SKILLS: Understanding Vocabulary in Context

Introduction

A. Cover the picture on the right with your hand and look at the picture on the left. Answer the questions. Then look at the picture on the right.

What is this? What is it for?   *Now can you guess?*

   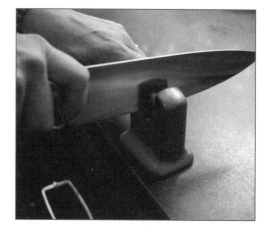

B. Why is the picture on the right easier to understand?

Reading Skill

Understanding vocabulary in context means understanding the meaning of a word from the other words around it—from its *context*.

Example

Happiness and anger are two important emotions.

You can try to understand the word emotions from the other words in the sentence. *Happiness* and *anger* help you understand the meaning of *emotions*.

Practice Understanding Vocabulary in Context

A. Work with a partner. Read the paragraph. Which words help you understand the meaning of the <u>underlined</u> words? Circle them. Then draw an arrow to connect them.

People don't always use words to express emotions. When we look at people's faces, we understand their feelings. People often use their faces, or facial expressions, to show their emotions. <u>Facial expressions</u> are <u>universal</u>—in every country of the world, a smile expresses happiness and a <u>frown</u> expresses sadness or anger.

B. Discuss the meanings of the underlined words with your classmates.

3 WORDS YOU NEED

Work with a partner. Read the statements. Use the context to guess the meaning of the <u>underlined</u> words and phrases. Then write the matching word or phrase next to the correct definition below.

1. "You never express your anger. That isn't healthy. It can even be <u>harmful</u> to your health."

2. "Don't be so angry. <u>Calm down</u>. Everything is OK."

3. "There are many <u>approaches</u> to solving problems. For example, some people talk it out. Other people ask for advice from experts."

4. "There's a problem. But we can <u>deal with</u> it. We can solve it."

a. _____ : ways to do something

b. _____ : to become less excited or angry

c. _____ : to do something about problems

d. _____ : able to hurt people

4 USE YOUR READING SKILLS

A. Preview the article on page 53 and make predictions. Answer the questions.

1. What is the topic of the article?
   a. ways to avoid anger
   b. ways to deal with anger
   c. ways to express all emotions

2. What will this article discuss? Mark your predictions with an **X**. As you read the article, check your predictions.

   ____ a. different approaches to anger

   ____ b. stories about when the writer was angry

   ____ c. the best way to deal with anger

   ____ d. the worst way to deal with anger

   ____ e. the best way to express emotions

B. These phrases are underlined in the article on page 53. As you read the article, look for their meanings in the context. Circle the meanings. After you read, write the meaning next to each phrase below.

1. anger-out _____

2. anger-in _____

3. controlled expression _____

4. anger management _____

This article from a health magazine discusses anger and some ways to deal with it.

Control Yourself!

Dealing with Anger in Everyday Life

Anger is not a "bad" emotion. It is really very normal. Most people get angry several times a week, and some people get angry several times a day.[1] Anger can even be helpful. For example, sometimes people have problems, but they don't realize[2] it—until they become angry. Their anger can help them see a problem and do something about it. So, anger is not a bad emotion, but people can express their anger in bad or harmful ways.

There are three main approaches to anger.[3] One approach is called *anger-out*. In

Anger-out approach

Anger-in approach

the anger-out approach, people express their anger in a very strong way. For example, they might yell,[4] say bad things, or even throw something. Another approach is called *anger-in*. With anger-in, people keep their angerinside them. They don't speak or behave in an angry way, but their anger doesn't go away.

Anger-out and anger-in are not good ways to deal with anger for two reasons. First, they are not useful for solving problems. When people only yell or only keep quiet, they are not communicating. Also, when people do not deal with anger well, their anger can have harmful results. Over time,

anger can cause serious health problems, such as high blood pressure, heart attack, or stroke.[5]

A better way to deal with anger is the *controlled expression* approach. In controlled expression, people calm down and think about their anger. When they express it, they express it in a helpful way. People can learn how to use controlled expression in *anger management* programs. Anger management teaches people to manage, or control, their anger. They learn to deal with their anger in helpful ways. For example, people learn to calm down, communicate better, and try to solve problems. They learn to avoid, not anger, but angry behavior.

Anger management programs help people understand anger and find a better way to deal with it. For people with anger problems, these programs can change anger from a "bad" emotion into a helpful, healthy emotion.

[1] This study is in J. R. Averill, "Studies on Anger and Aggression: Implications for Theories of Emotion," *American Psychologist*, 38 (1983: 1145–1160).

[2] **realize:** to understand

[3] Studies on approaches to anger are from the University of Michigan School of Public Health.

[4] **yell:** to speak in a very loud and angry way

[5] **high blood pressure, heart attack, stroke:** serious problems of the blood, heart, and brain

6 UNDERSTAND THE READING

A. For each question, circle *one or more* answers.

1. When Jana gets angry, she usually yells. What is her approach to anger?

    a. anger-out
    b. anger-in
    c. controlled expression

2. When Malik gets angry, he almost never yells. What is his approach to anger?

    a. anger-out
    b. anger-in
    c. controlled expression

3. Which approach to anger can cause health problems?

    a. anger-out
    b. anger-in
    c. controlled expression

4. Which approach to anger do anger management classes teach?

    a. anger-out
    b. anger-in
    c. controlled expression

B. Look back at the quiz on page 50. Take the quiz again using the information from the article .

C. Work in a small group. Discuss these questions.

1. When was anger helpful to you?

2. When was anger harmful to you?

3. Are anger management programs a good idea? Why or why not?

WORK WITH THE VOCABULARY

A. Complete the sentences with a word or phrase from the box.

| a. approaches | b. calm down | c. deal with | d. harmful |

1. There are three main ____ to anger.

2. Anger-out and anger-in are not good ways to ____ anger.

3. The ____ results of anger include serious health problems.

4. Anger management programs help people learn to ____ and solve problems.

SUFFIXES: -ful

You can use the suffix -ful to form adjectives from some nouns.

Noun: success   The program has a lot of success.
Adjective: successful   The program is very successful.

B. Use -ful to form adjectives from the nouns. Work with a partner to write a sample sentence for each adjective. Share your sentences with your classmates.

1. Noun	use	There are good uses for anger.
Adjective		
2. Noun	help	His advice was a big help to me.
Adjective		
3. Noun	harm	Anger can cause harm to your health.
Adjective		

8 GET READY TO READ ABOUT: Anger Management

A. **Which words do you know? Put an X next to these words. Ask your classmates about the other words, or look them up in a dictionary.**

___ breathe   ___ relax   ___ form (*v.*)

___ manage   ___ expert   ___ lesson

B. **Read the schedule for an anger management class. Look at the items above the schedule. Put them under the correct topic in the schedule.**

~~Listen to the other person.~~

Breathe deeply.

Ask for advice from experts.

Think in a slow and careful way.

Don't interrupt.

Think of solutions, not problems.

Class Schedule
June 7: Better communication
• *Listen to the other person.*
• _____
June 14: Problem solving
• _____
• _____
June 21: The moment of anger: Keep calm!
• _____
• _____

9 WORDS YOU NEED

Look at the underlined words. Use the context—the pictures and other words—to guess their meanings. Discuss your guesses with a partner.

10 USE YOUR READING SKILLS

A. Preview the story on page 58 and make predictions. Answer the questions.

1. Who are the two people in the pictures? Circle your answer.

   a. two teachers
   b. two students
   c. a teacher and a student

2. What will happen in this story? Mark your predictions with an **X**.
   As you read the story, check your predictions.

   ____ a. a teacher and a student have a misunderstanding

   ____ b. a teacher and a student have a fight

   ____ c. students discuss their lesson after class

   ____ d. teachers discuss the students after class

   ____ e. a teacher and a student discuss something after class

B. These words and the phrase are underlined in the article on page 58. As you read the article, look for their meanings in the context. Circle the meanings. After you read, write the meaning next to each one below.

1. jump to conclusions _____

2. stared _____

3. embarrassed _____

An anger management teacher wrote and illustrated this story for a teaching newsletter. She forgot her own lessons—until a student reminded her of them.

The Teacher Learns a Lesson
by Sandra Chin

I'm an anger management expert, so I manage my anger well—right? Not always! I want to share a story about a lesson from my anger management class. I feel a little uncomfortable about it, a little embarrassed, because a student taught[1] this lesson to me—the teacher!

Last week, the topic was *The Moment of Anger: Keep Calm!* I taught my students: Never jump to conclusions—don't form an opinion about a situation too quickly. You might get the wrong idea and get angry for no reason. When you start to feel angry, breathe deeply and think in a slow and careful way. This will help you keep calm and stop you from jumping to conclusions. All the students were very interested in the lesson—all except[2] one student, Peter.

I looked at Peter, but he never looked at me. He stared at the wall—just looked at the wall for a long time. He wasn't paying any attention. Soon, he started to write something on a piece of paper. "What is he writing?" I thought.[3] "It's a note to his girlfriend!" Then I felt[4] *very* angry.

At the end of class, I said, "Peter, I need to talk to you."

"I want to talk to you, too," Peter said. "This class was great! Sometimes I jump to conclusions, and this will help me stop. I wrote down a lot of ideas! . . . What do you want to tell me?"

"Uh, nothing," I said. "Good night, Peter."

"Oh, OK. Well, thanks for the class. I really learned a lot," Peter said.

I was so embarrassed. Peter was taking notes, not writing to his girlfriend. He was staring at the wall, but he was also paying attention. I taught my students to think carefully before forming an opinion, but I didn't. I jumped to conclusions! I taught my students to calm down, but I didn't. I got[5] angry.

Keep calm and don't jump to conclusions. Peter learned these lessons from me, and I learned these lessons—my own lessons—from him.

---

[1] **taught:** past tense of *teach*
[2] **except:** but not
[3] **thought (v.):** the past tense of *think*
[4] **felt (v.):** the past tense of *feel*
[5] **got:** past tense of *get*

12 UNDERSTAND THE READING

A. Circle the correct word or phrase for each sentence.

Last week the teacher discussed (1) <u>jumping to conclusions / breathing deeply</u>. This week the topic was (2) <u>listening to the other person / keeping calm</u>. She didn't follow her own advice. She felt (3) <u>sad / angry</u> because of a student. The student was (4) <u>staring at the wall / staring at the teacher</u>. She thought, (5) <u>"He's not paying attention." / "He's not coming to class often enough."</u> The student was (6) <u>writing to his girlfriend / taking notes</u>, but the teacher didn't know it. When she realized the true situation, she felt (7) <u>embarrassed / angry</u>.

B. Work in a small group. Discuss the questions.

1. Why was the teacher in the story on page 58 embarrassed?

2. When you get angry, do you ever count to 10 or breathe deeply? Do you use other techniques to keep calm? What are they?

13 WORK WITH THE VOCABULARY

Circle the correct answer.

1. When a person is embarrassed, she feels ____ .
   a. a little silly or stupid
   b. very angry
   c. happy and friendly

2. When a person jumps to conclusions, she ____ .
   a. decides something slowly and carefully
   b. decides something quickly, without thinking
   c. thinks carefully but can't make a decision

3. When a person stares at something, he ____ .
   a. closes his eyes and seems to sleep
   b. writes in a notebook very quickly
   c. looks at something for a long time

14 GET READY TO READ AND SHARE

Work with a partner. Complete the chart with the missing words about men and women. Check your answers with your classmates.

👩	👨
Girl	Boy
	Son
	Man
Female	
Feminine = about a woman, like a woman; right for a woman	Masculine =

15 USE YOUR READING SKILLS

A. You are going to read one part of a magazine article about some differences between men and women. Read the beginning of the article below. Then answer the questions.

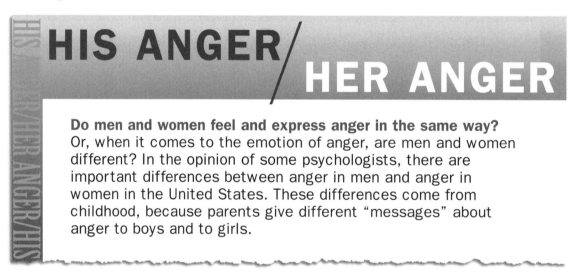

HIS ANGER / HER ANGER

Do men and women feel and express anger in the same way? Or, when it comes to the emotion of anger, are men and women different? In the opinion of some psychologists, there are important differences between anger in men and anger in women in the United States. These differences come from childhood, because parents give different "messages" about anger to boys and to girls.

1. Do men and women in the U.S. express anger differently?

2. Where do "messages" about anger come from?

B. Preview Part A and Part B of the article on pages 61 and 62. Then answer these questions.

1. What is men's approach to anger? a. express it strongly b. keep it inside
2. What is women's approach to anger? a. express it strongly b. keep it inside

Now choose one part of the article to read. Read Part A on page 61 <u>or</u> Part B on page 62.

MEN:
An "Anger-Out" Approach

HIS ANGER/HER ANGER/HIS ANGER/HER ANGER/HIS ANGER/HER ANGER/HIS ANGER/HER

Sons learn how to deal with anger from their parents. They learn from their parents' words and actions. Parents in the United States tell their sons not to cry. The message to boys is this: Don't feel afraid, hurt, or sad. So when boys feel these emotions, they learn not to express them. When boys are angry and fight with their friends, their parents don't tell them to stop. The message is: Anger and fighting are masculine. They are OK for boys.

These childhood messages influence adult feelings and behavior. When boys become adults, they sometimes have difficulty expressing fear,[1] hurt, or sadness. They often are more comfortable with expressing feelings of anger. For example, when something bad happens, they might use an anger-out approach. They might yell or throw things.

There are positive and negative sides to the anger-out approach. On the positive side, many men are able to express their anger. This is good, because it is helpful to express anger. On the negative side, it is not helpful to yell and throw things. It is also not healthy to keep feelings such as fear, hurt, or sadness inside.

Men need to understand when their anger is helpful and when it is harmful. Then they can control their anger and send better messages to their own sons.

[1] **fear:** the feeling of being afraid

Who can answer these questions about Part A with you? Find a partner. Answer the questions.

Focus Questions

1. What messages do boys get?

2. Which emotions are difficult for men to express? Which emotion is easier?

3. What is the positive side of expressing anger for men? What is the negative side?

WOMEN:
An "Anger-In" Approach

Daughters learn how to deal with anger from their parents. They learn from the parents' words and actions. Parents in the United States let girls show many emotions, including fear,[1] hurt, and sadness. They let girls cry. The message is: It is OK to express emotions. Then they tell their daughters: Anger is not a nice emotion, and girls should always be nice. When girls are angry and fight with friends, their parents tell them to stop. The message is: Anger and fighting are *not* feminine. They are *not* OK for girls.

These childhood messages influence adult feelings and behavior. When girls become adults, they can usually express fear, hurt, or sadness, but sometimes they have difficulty expressing anger. For example, when something makes them angry, they might use an anger-in approach. They might keep all their anger inside and not express it.

There are positive and negative sides to the anger-in approach. On the positive side, many women are comfortable expressing fear, sadness, and many other emotions. This is good, because it is helpful to express emotions. On the negative side, some women have difficulty expressing anger, and that is not healthy. It can even be harmful to their health.

Women need to learn to express their anger in helpful ways. Then they can be healthier and also send better messages to their own daughters.

[1] **fear:** the feeling of being afraid

Who can answer these questions about Part B with you? Find a partner. Answer the questions.

Focus Questions

1. What messages do girls get?

2. Which emotions are easy for women to express? Which emotion is more difficult?

3. What is the positive side of expressing anger for women? What is the negative side?

Organize Your Thoughts

Work with your partner.
Part A readers: Complete the chart on the left.
Part B readers: Complete the chart on the right.
All readers: Complete the bottom chart with information from your part of
the article.

Boys get the message, this is OK:

_____

_____

Boys get the message, this is not OK:

_____

_____

Men express this easily:

_____

_____

Men express this with difficulty:

_____

_____

Girls get the message, this is OK:

_____

_____

Girls get the message, this is not OK:

_____

_____

Women express this easily:

_____

_____

Women express this with difficulty:

_____

_____

Some men/women need to do this:

_____

_____

Share Your Information

Who can tell you about the other part of the article? Find a pair of classmates.

1. With your partner, tell the other pair about your information. Use the charts.

2. Add some other details from your part of the article.

Share Your Ideas

Discuss the question with your partner and the other pair. Then share your answers with the class.

Think about the men and women you know, including yourself. Do they express anger in different ways? Explain your answer and give examples.

18 REFLECT ON: Keeping Calm

A. Read these questions. Then read one student's answers.

1. Think of a time when you were angry. Why were you angry?

2. How did you express your anger? What did you do?

3. What happened?

4. Did you deal with your anger well? Why or why not?

> When I started my new job last year, I felt angry almost every afternoon from 4:00 to 5:30. I felt angry because I was driving home from work and there was always so much traffic. The trip is only 20 minutes with no traffic, but it was one and a half hours with traffic! I didn't really express my anger, but every day I felt upset. So I decided not to drive to work. Now, I take the bus. It is better for me not to drive to work. When I'm not driving, I'm not angry.

B. In a small group, discuss these questions.

1. Why was the writer angry every day from 4:00 to 5:30?

2. Did this student deal with her anger well? Why or why not?

C. Now write your own paragraph. Answer the questions in A. Then add some details. You can use the student's paragraph as a model.

Unit 5

The Business of Beauty

In this unit, you are going to:
- read about beauty in the U.S.
- learn how to preview headings

WHAT DO YOU KNOW ABOUT THE BUSINESS OF BEAUTY?

A. Work with a partner. Name the businesses in this picture. Why do people go to these businesses? Which of these businesses do you go to?

B. Think about the questions. Discuss your answers with your classmates.

1. Look again at the picture above. Which of these types of businesses were also popular twenty years ago? Fifty years ago?

2. Who spends more money today on beauty—men or women, young adults or older adults? Was this different in the past?

3. Are there more beauty businesses now than in the past? Why or why not?

1 GET READY TO READ ABOUT: Ideas About Female Beauty

A. Look at the pictures of women's fashion in the U.S. from different time periods. What differences do you see? Discuss your answers with a partner. Then share your answers with your classmates.

B. Think about women today. What is the ideal of female beauty today? Is there only one? Discuss your answers with your classmates.

2 BUILD YOUR READING SKILLS: Previewing Headings

Introduction

A. Look at Picture A. Why is this shopper having problems? Then look at Picture B. Why is it easier for the shopper to find things now?

B. The signs over the aisles in Picture B are similar to headings in a text. Look at the sample text on page 67. How do the headings make it easier to find information?

Reading Skill

> **Previewing headings** gives you information about the parts of a text. The title tells you the topic of the whole text; the headings tell you the topic of each part.

Practice Previewing Headings

Preview the article. Then look at the predictions below. Mark your predictions with an X.

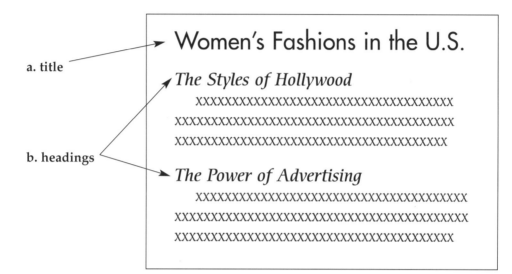

This article might discuss . . .

_____ **1.** the influence of French fashion in the U.S.

_____ **2.** the influence of movies on fashion in the U.S.

_____ **3.** the influence of TV commercials on fashion in the U.S.

_____ **4.** the influence of magazine ads on fashion in the U.S.

_____ **5.** the influence of price on fashion in the U.S.

WORDS YOU NEED

Read the advertisement. Then guess definitions of the words below.

Natalia's Beauty Institute

How do you want to look? What is your <u>ideal</u>? You can have this perfect <u>look</u>! Take classes at Natalia's Beauty Institute and learn how to look beautiful!

This week's class: *Beauty Through Cosmetics*
How can you make your eyes, your lips, your skin more beautiful?
Learn to choose and use the right <u>cosmetics</u>.
You can <u>create</u> a beautiful new face!

Next week: *Thin Is In!*
Learn how to lose weight and get a <u>thin</u> body for summer!

____ **1.** create   a. a perfect example of a person or thing

____ **2.** ideal (*n.*)   b. products to use on your face to look good

____ **3.** cosmetics   c. style, fashion

____ **4.** look (*n.*)   d. not fat

____ **5.** thin   e. to make something very special

4 **USE YOUR READING SKILLS**

A. **Preview the article on page 69. Look at the title, the introductory material, the pictures, the captions, and the headings. Circle your answers.**

1. What is the topic of the article?

   a. art in the U.S.
   b. famous American movie stars
   c. American ideas about beauty for women

2. What do the headings tell you about?

   a. different regions in the U.S.
   b. different time periods in the U.S.
   c. different ages of women in the U.S.

B. **Use your preview to make predictions about the text. Circle your answers. As you read the article, check your predictions.**

1. American women over the years (did/did not) think about their looks.

2. Fashions changed, and the ideal female body also (changed/stayed the same).

For women in the U.S. in the 20th Century, the ideal of beauty changed many times. This article from a fashion magazine tells about these changes.

Fashion

American Beauty

The 20th century was a time of great change in the U.S. With every change in the country, the ideal of female beauty also changed. Fashion, cosmetics, and advertising companies influenced these changes. They gave[1] women new ideals to dream about, and lots of new products to buy.

The Early 20th Century

Early in the century, Charles Dana Gibson, an artist, created the "Gibson Girl." The Gibson Girl was tall and thin, and her hair was high on top of her head. She wore[2] a long skirt with a very small waist. Women looked at Gibson Girl pictures in magazine ads. They liked this ideal and wanted to match it. They wanted to buy clothes and style their hair like the pictures.

In the 1920s women had more freedom,[3] so the ideal changed to match. For the first time, hair and skirts were short. The ideal—the *flapper*—was thin and boyish.[4] In magazines and movies, flappers wore make-up. Women started to use the same makeup, and cosmetics companies started to grow!

Mid 20th Century

When American men returned from World War II, many people married and started families. At this time, a curvy, soft body was the ideal. The fashion was tight sweaters and skirts with small waists. Women used a lot of make-up and beauty products. Movie star Marilyn Monroe fit the ideal perfectly.

At this time, advertising started to have a greater influence because of television. TV commercials used ideals of female beauty to sell many types of products—cosmetics, cleaning products, and cars!

Late 20th Century and Today

In the 1960s and 70s, young people wanted to try a different kind of life. Young women wanted more freedom. In clothing, jeans were the fashion. In cosmetics, the "natural" look was popular—less makeup and straight hair. The ideal body was thin again.

At the end of twentieth century, there wasn't just one ideal of female beauty. This is also true today. Women usually find their own style now. With so many choices today, each woman can be her own ideal!

[1] **gave:** past tense of *give*
[2] **wore:** past tense of *wear*
[3] **freedom:** the ability to say and do the things you want
[4] **boyish:** similar to a boy

6 UNDERSTAND THE READING

A. Match the ideal to the time period.

Time period

_____ 1. the early 20th century

_____ 2. the 1920s

_____ 3. after World War II

_____ 4. the 1960s and 70s

_____ 5. late 20th century and today

Ideal

a. tight sweaters and curvy bodies

b. the Gibson Girl

c. the natural look

d. many different looks and styles

e. thin and boyish

B. Circle the correct word in each sentence.

1. The Gibson Girl was tall, confident, and (thin/natural).

2. Flappers wore their hair and their skirts (tall/short).

3. Women used the make-up, and the (advertising/cosmetics) industry started to grow.

4. After World War II, advertising started to have a greater influence because of (television/cosmetics).

5. In the 1960s and 70s, the "natural" look was popular—less (freedom/make-up) and straight hair.

6. With so many choices today, each woman can be her own (movie star/ideal)!

C. Work in a small group. Discuss the questions.

1. What are the fashions for women today?

2. Is beauty more or less important in the lives of women today?

3. What are the fashions for men today? Do fashions for men change?

4. Who or what influences your ideas about beauty and fashion? How?

7 WORK WITH THE VOCABULARY

A. In each word set, three words belong together. One word does not belong. Cross out that word.

1. thin	~~popular~~	tall	soft
2. skirt	jeans	short	dress
3. advertising	influence	cosmetics	fashion
4. beauty	ideal	look	make-up

B. Complete the sentences with a word from the box.

a. cosmetics	b. create	c. ideals	d. look	e. thin

1. The Gibson Girl was tall and ____, and her hair was high on top of her head.

2. TV commercials used ____ of female beauty to sell many types of products.

3. In the 1960s and 70s, the natural ____ was popular—less make-up and straight hair.

4. In the 1920s, women started to use make-up, and ____ companies started to grow.

5. Women today have many choices. They usually ____ their own style.

C. Choose two of the words from the box in B above. Write a sentence about your own life for each one. Then share your sentences with your classmates.

_____

_____

_____

_____

_____

_____

A. Take the quiz about modeling. Put an X under True or False. Check your answers in the answer key.

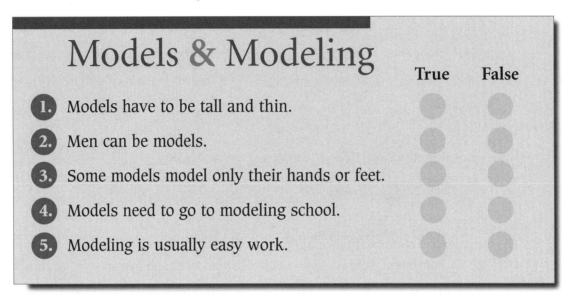

Models & Modeling

		True	False
1.	Models have to be tall and thin.		
2.	Men can be models.		
3.	Some models model only their hands or feet.		
4.	Models need to go to modeling school.		
5.	Modeling is usually easy work.		

B. Match the words to the items in the picture. Check your answers with a partner.

1. camera ____   2. finger ____   3. hand ____

4. gloves ____   5. jewelry ____   6. model ____

7. nails ____   8. nail polish ____   9. photographer ____

9 WORDS YOU NEED

Read the job center information card on modeling. With a partner, guess the words with a similar meaning to the underlined words. Circle them.

Career: The Job of Modeling

Work description:

A model stands and moves to show clothing or products. He or she works with a photographer in photo shoots, for distance shots and close-up shots.

Getting started in this career:

- Have a resume and a portfolio of photographs. The portfolio should include photographs from modeling jobs.
- An agent is useful. This person can find work for you in magazines, advertising companies, and other businesses.

10 USE YOUR READING SKILLS

A. Preview the article on page 74. Look at the title, the introductory material, the pictures, the captions, and the headings. Circle your answer.

What is the topic of the article?

 a. Kara Moore's career as a hand model
 b. Kara Moore's opinion of hand modeling
 c. Kara Moore's search for a hand modeling job

B. Use your preview to make predictions. Mark your predictions with an X. As you read the article, check your predictions.

Which questions does the article answer?

____ a. Is Kara Moore married and does she have children?

____ b. Does Kara Moore know famous models?

____ c. How does Kara Moore take care of her hands?

____ d. Is Kara Moore's work difficult?

____ e. How can readers take care of their hands?

This article in a teen magazine is an interview with an unusual type of model.

Working with Her Hands

By Jamal Edwards

Last week I was in a cafeteria. The woman at the next table had gloves on, and she never removed them. She even had lunch with them on. I needed to know the reason for this, so I asked her. She laughed and explained, "I'm a hand model!" I wanted to know more. This week, hand model Kara Moore sits down for an interview with *Need To Know* magazine and tells me all about it.

The Life of a Hand Model

Need To Know: Hi, Kara. Thanks for making time to talk to me.

Kara Moore: I'm happy to! This is fun.

NTK: First, explain something for our readers. What do hand models do?

KM: Usually, we work in magazine ads and TV commercials. My hands are in ads for dishwashing soap, nail polish, watches, jewelry. . . all kinds of products.

Kara Moore, hand model

NTK: Do you ever work in movies?

KM: Sure. Some actresses have bad hands, unattractive hands. Sometimes they need a close-up shot of her hands doing something. They shoot, or take pictures of, my hands instead.

NTK: So tell me—to be a hand model, are beautiful hands enough?

KM: Beautiful hands are just the start! It takes a long time to learn how to do this well. You have to build a portfolio and keep[1] calling your agent. At photo shoots, you need to pay attention and keep still[2] for a long time. You also need to get along well with the photographer and all the people at the photo shoot. All day, every day, you have to be very careful and take good care of your hands.

Hand Care Advice from a Professional

NTK: Kara, a lot of our readers want to know. . . How do you take care of your hands?

KM: As you know, Jamal, I wear gloves most of the time. One scratch or broken nail, and I can lose a job.

Kara at work

NTK: Do you avoid certain things?

KM: Housework is very bad for the hands! Also, I'm always careful. Usually, people don't think about their hands. I think about my hands all the time.

NTK: And what do you do to make your hands beautiful?

KM: I always use sunscreen[3] and moisturizers[4] on my hands and nails. I also get help from hand and nail experts. I even do hand exercises!

NTK: Kara, before we finish, do you have any advice on hand care for our readers?

KM: Take care of your hands. You only have two of them!

---

[1] **keep:** to continue
[2] **keep still:** to not move
[3] **sunscreen:** a product to protect skin from the sun
[4] **moisturizer:** a product to help skin feel less dry

12 UNDERSTAND THE READING

A. Match the beginning of the sentences to the correct end of the sentences.

____ **1.** Hand models work in commercials   a. when actresses have ugly hands.

____ **2.** In a photo shoot, models have to   b. build a portfolio.

____ **3.** To take care of their hands, hand models   c. keep still for a long time.

____ **4.** Hand models work in movies   d. wear gloves and avoid housework.

____ **5.** To find good jobs, hand models need to   e. for soaps, nail polish, and jewelry.

B. Work in a small group. Discuss these questions.

1. Is modeling interesting work? Why or why not?

2. Imagine you want to be a hand model. Think about your usual activities. Which activities will you have to avoid or change?

13 WORK WITH THE VOCABULARY

Read Kara Moore's story about her life as a hand model. Complete her story with words from the box.

a. career   **c.** housework   **e.** photographer

b. fashion   **d.** natural   **f.** scratch

Yesterday, I stayed home and did ____. When I finished, my apartment
        ₁
was clean and I felt happy. But then I noticed a ____ on my hand! At that
            ₂
moment the phone rang. It was my agent, and she had a job for me!

"A famous ____ is taking pictures for a ____ magazine, and he wants
      ₃   ₄
you! Don't wear nail polish. He wants a ____ look for this photo. This job will
            ₅
be very good for your ____."
      ₆
I wanted the job, but I thought, "Oh, no! The scratch!" Luckily, they
needed a perfect right hand, and the scratch was on my left hand. The job
was mine!

14 GET READY TO READ AND SHARE

Read the advertisement. Then discuss the questions below with your classmates.

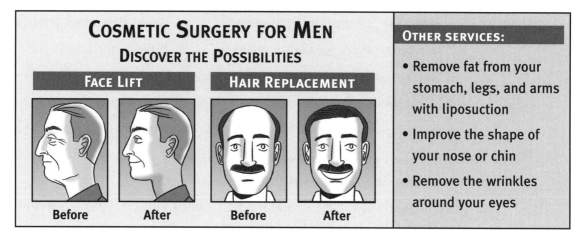

1. Think about the men you know. Are they interested in cosmetic surgery? Why or why not?

2. What is your opinion of cosmetic surgery for men? Why?

15 USE YOUR READING SKILLS

A. You are going to read one part of an article from a men's health magazine. Read the beginning of the article below. Then answer the questions.

Healthy Man Magazine ARE YOU *FOR* OR *AGAINST* COSMETIC SURGERY FOR MEN?

Cosmetic surgery today is becoming easier, cheaper, and more popular with men. A lot of men have questions about cosmetic surgery. *Healthy Man Magazine* asked two men to present their opinions. Raj Singh is a lawyer from Portland, Oregon. He deals with public health problems. Alain Duchamp is a businessman from Tampa, Florida. He also volunteers as a job counselor for business school students. Here are their arguments for and against cosmetic surgery for men.

1. How is cosmetic surgery changing?

2. Who will present opinions in this article?

B. Preview Part A and Part B of the magazine article on pages 77 and 78. Then answer the questions.

1. What is Raj Singh's opinion of cosmetic surgery?   for   against

2. What is Alain Duchamp's opinion of cosmetic surgery?   for   against

Now choose one part of the article to read. Read Part A on page 77 *or* Part B on page 78.

The Wrong Approach
Raj Singh

Attitudes about cosmetic surgery are changing, and this is not a good thing. Cosmetic surgery is very popular today, but it still isn't safe. It isn't the same as getting a new haircut or coloring your hair! Surgery is surgery—it can be dangerous and has many risks.[1] People should avoid surgery—any kind of surgery.

Health risks are the most important reason not to get cosmetic surgery, but there are many others. After cosmetic surgery, people sometimes look unnatural.[2] They want to look better but instead they look worse. Also, some cosmetic surgery is very expensive. There are much better ways to spend your money.

People talk about the need for cosmetic surgery in the business world. This is their idea: Good looks help you, or give you an advantage. After a face-lift or liposuction, men feel better about themselves. They have more confidence. This may be true, but cosmetic surgery is the wrong approach. Confidence—not good looks—is the real advantage.

Men, you don't need cosmetic surgery to have more confidence. Accept[3] your big nose! Love your wrinkles! Go outside and exercise. Feel good about your healthy body, and don't think so much about your looks. Confidence will improve your life more than any cosmetic surgery.

[1] **risk (n.):** the possibility of something bad happening
[2] **unnatural:** not natural
[3] **accept:** decide something is OK

Who can answer these questions about Part A with you? Find a partner. Answer the questions.

Focus Questions
1. What are the risks of cosmetic surgery?
2. According to Mr. Singh, what are some ways for men to get more confidence?
3. Find the word "advantage" in paragraph 3. Look at the context. What does "advantage" mean?

Cosmetic Surgery *Can* Help
Alain Duchamp

Attitudes about cosmetic surgery are different now for a good reason. Cosmetic surgery is different, and the world is different.

Negative opinions about cosmetic surgery are really about cosmetic surgery in the past. People with negative opinions don't understand the changes in cosmetic surgery. Cosmetic surgery today is easier, cheaper, and better. Every year, doctors improve their skills, and now risks[1] are small.

Cosmetic surgery helps people look better. When they look better, they feel better. Men exercise, go on diets to lose weight, color their hair, buy new clothes. Why is cosmetic surgery any different? Why is hair coloring OK, but not hair replacement? This doesn't make sense.[2]

Men, the best reason for cosmetic surgery is your career. Today's work world is very competitive.[3] Your looks influence people's opinion of you. Maybe this isn't a good thing, but it's true. Cosmetic surgery can help you, or give you an advantage. It can give you more hair, take away wrinkles, and make you look better. These changes make you feel better about yourself and give you more confidence. This confidence is the real advantage.

[1] **risk:** the possibility of something bad happening
[2] **doesn't make sense:** isn't good thinking
[3] **competitive:** difficult to do well in

Who can answer these questions about Part B with you? Find a partner. Answer the questions.

Focus Questions

1. How is cosmetic surgery different today?

2. According to Mr. Duchamp, what is good about cosmetic surgery?

3. Find the word "advantage" in paragraph 4. Look at the context. What does "advantage" mean?

Organize Your Thoughts

Work with your partner. Complete the chart with information from your part of the article. Circle the writer's opinion. Then give three reasons for this opinion.

Opinion:
a. Cosmetic surgery is good.
b. Cosmetic surgery is bad.
Reasons for opinion:
1.
2.
3.

Share Your Information

Who can tell you about the other part of the article? With your partner, find another pair of classmates.

1. With your partner, share your answers from the chart above with the other pair of students.

2. Add details to support the writer's opinion.

Share Your Ideas

Discuss these questions with your partner and the other pair of students. Then share your answers with your classmates.

1. Which opinion about cosmetic surgery for men do you agree with?

2. Do you feel differently about cosmetic surgery for women? Why or why not?

18 REFLECT ON: Beauty

A. Read these questions. Then read one student's answer.

1. Do people think too much about their looks? Explain.

2. Do people spend too much time and money on beauty and fashion? Explain.

3. Do ads for clothing and beauty products influence people? If yes, how much do they influence people?

People don't think too much about their looks. My friends and I think about our looks, but this is normal and fun. We like fashion, and we buy fashion magazines. We like to buy nice clothes. When I look good, I feel good, and I feel happy. Ads don't influence me too much. They give me good ideas, but I make my own decisions.

B. In a small group, discuss the questions.

1. Do you agree with some or all of this student's opinions? Which ones? Why do you agree?

2. Is this student typical or unusual? Why?

3. What are your answers to the questions in A?

C. Now write your own paragraph. Answer the questions in A. Then add some details. You can use the student's paragraph as a model.

Unit 6

Finding the Right Balance

In this unit, you are going to:
- read about finding the right balance in life in the U.S.
- learn to use comprehension questions to preview a text

WHAT DO YOU KNOW ABOUT FINDING A GOOD BALANCE IN LIFE?

A. Look at the picture. Which student has a better balance in her life? Which student is more like you? Discuss your answers with your classmates.

I do my homework quickly the morning before class.

I hurry to class and eat a sandwich on the way.

I have too much work. I can never relax.

I never take vacations. I don't have enough time.

Sonya

I study a little bit every afternoon.

I sit down for 15 minutes and eat a quick lunch.

I work a lot, but I find time for fun.

I try to take a vacation every year.
It helps me relax.

Linda

B. Read the questions and circle your answers. Discuss your answers with your classmates.

1. How do you like to study?

   a. I like to do homework and study for exams at the last minute.
   b. I like to do homework and study for exams a little every day.

2. What is your ideal work situation?

   a. work during the day and have time for fun activities in the evening
   b. work at night and have time for fun activities during the day
   c. work at home, and mix work with fun activities all day

3. What is your ideal vacation?

   a. to be relaxed and lazy all day every day
   b. to be active all day every day
   c. to have some active time and some lazy time

GET READY TO READ ABOUT: Finding the Right Balance in a Camping Vacation

A. Look at the picture. How is camping different for each person. How is it the same? Discuss your answers with your classmates.

B. Match the camping items and activities to the typical travel items and activities. Check your answers with a partner.

____ **1.** tent (*n.*)   a. bed

____ **2.** campfire   b. suitcase

____ **3.** sleeping bag   c. hotel, motel

____ **4.** trail   d. walk (*v.*)

____ **5.** hike (*v.*)   e. sidewalk

____ **6.** backpack (*n.*)   f. microwave

C. Work with your partner. You are planning a camping trip. Complete these two lists. Share your answers with your classmates.

Things to Take	Fun Things to Do
1. tent	**1.** swim
2.	**2.**
3.	**3.**
4.	**4.**

2 BUILD YOUR READING SKILLS: Previewing Comprehension Questions

Introduction

A. Look at the picture. Why is the announcer asking questions? Discuss this with your classmates.

Where can you camp? What should you take? Does camping cost a lot? Today's program answers these questions.

B. The announcer's questions are like the comprehension questions at the end of a text. How can comprehension questions help you make predictions about a text?

Reading Skill

Comprehension questions are usually at the end of a text. They help you check how well you understand the text. Before you read a text, preview the comprehension questions. Then as you read the text, <u>underline</u> the answers to the questions.

Practice Previewing Comprehension Questions

Read the comprehension questions below and then read the text. Underline the answers to the comprehension questions as you read.

> **Camping**
> You want to go camping. Your first question is: Where can I camp? There are three kinds of campgrounds in the United States: <u>campgrounds in national parks</u>, campgrounds in state parks, and private campgrounds. The U.S. government runs campgrounds in national parks. States run campgrounds in state parks. And companies run private campgrounds.

1. What are the three kinds of campgrounds in the U.S.?

2. Who runs the campgrounds in national parks?

3. Who runs private campgrounds?

3 WORDS YOU NEED

Read the sentences. Guess the meaning of the underlined words. Check your answers after you read the article on page 133.

1. We went camping because we wanted to be closer to <u>nature</u>.
   a. mountains, trees, rivers
   b. houses, offices, stores
   c. buses, trains, cars

2. This hiking trail is very hard, but that's OK. I like <u>challenges</u>.
   a. silly but fun activities
   b. difficult but interesting activities
   c. old but true activities

3. I don't like to camp. I like the <u>comforts</u> of home—a soft bed, a shower, a refrigerator.
   a. things to make life easier
   b. things to decorate your home
   c. things to help you clean

4. My daughter's job is to hike the trails and help people. That's not my job. For me, hiking is only <u>recreational</u>.
   a. for education
   b. for fun
   c. for money

4 USE YOUR READING SKILLS

A. Preview the article on page 85. Answer the questions.

1. What is the topic of the reading?

   _____

2. What are the three types of camping?

   _____

   _____

   _____

B. Preview the comprehension questions on page 86 and predict the answers. As you read the article, underline the answers in the text.

This article from the travel section of the newspaper is about finding the right balance of comfort and challenge in a camping vacation.

TravelNews

THE CHALLENGES AND COMFORTS OF CAMPING
Which Balance Is Right for You?

Camping vacations help people relax and enjoy nature, but people relax in different ways. Luckily, there are different kinds of camping in the United States. Each offers a different balance of comfort and challenge.

Recreational camping

Recreational camping lets you experience the beauty of nature and also have many comforts. Recreational campers usually camp in RVs (recreational vehicles) and stay at private campgrounds. This kind of camping can cost a lot. RVs are expensive to buy, but you can rent one for much less money.

Some RVs have all the comforts of home—nice kitchens, bathrooms, living rooms with TVs, and much more. With recreational camping, you can hike, swim, and fish all day and then relax with a movie in the evening.

Tent camping

You don't need an RV to go camping. You can use a tent. Tent campers usually stay at campgrounds in national and state parks. These campgrounds usually have buildings with bathrooms and showers for campers to share. Most tent campers cook their own meals over a campfire or on a camp stove.

Tent camping is great for families and beginning campers. It combines[1] some challenges with some comforts. Tent camping is less expensive, but you need to buy some equipment—for example, a tent, sleeping bags, and a camp stove.

Wilderness camping

With wilderness[2] camping, there are few comforts, no electricity, and no bathrooms. Wilderness campers don't stay in campgrounds with other people. They go off alone in national or state parks or special "wilderness areas." They carry their own food and equipment, and they sleep in tents or sometimes under the stars.

Sometimes wilderness campers have to deal with the risks and challenges of extreme[3] weather or wild animals. Because there are more risks, wilderness camping is for experienced campers—it is not a good idea for beginners.

Recreational, tent, and wilderness camping each offers a different balance of challenge and comfort. When you plan your camping vacation, choose the right balance for you.

[1] **combine:** to put together
[2] **wilderness:** area of land with no people, often with many trees and animals
[3] **extreme:** very strong or bad

6 UNDERSTAND THE READING

A. **Circle the correct answers. For some questions, *more than one* answer is correct.**

1. Which type of camping can you usually find at private campgrounds?

   a. recreational camping
   b. tent camping
   c. wilderness camping

2. In which type of camping do campers sleep in tents?

   a. recreational camping
   b. tent camping
   c. wilderness camping

3. Which type of camping usually offers campers shared bathrooms and showers?

   a. recreational camping
   b. tent camping
   c. wilderness camping

4. Which type of camping has the most risks?

   a. recreational camping
   b. tent camping
   c. wilderness camping

5. Which type of camping offers a balance of comfort and challenge?

   a. recreational camping
   b. tent camping
   c. wilderness camping

B. **Work in a small group. Imagine the situation and discuss your answers. Then share your ideas with your classmates.**

You worked really hard this year. Now it's summer and you're planning a camping vacation. You can do any kind of camping. Think about the different balances of challenge and comfort. Which type of camping do you want to do? Why?

7 WORK WITH THE VOCABULARY

A. Complete the e-mail message with the words in the box. Use each word one time.

| a. challenges | b. comforts | c. nature | d. recreational | e. supplies |

From: Suzanna Viera
To: Alexa Franklin
Subject: Our family vacation

Hey, Alexa! Your vacation on the beach sounds so relaxing! We're planning our vacation now. Our vacation doesn't sound relaxing.

Last year we went on a _____ camping trip. We
                                    1
rented an RV and stayed in a beautiful campground. That RV had lots of

_____, including air conditioning and a DVD player. I loved
          2
it! This year, the kids want more _____. For them, a
                                              3
vacation in _____ isn't enough. They want a vacation in the
                    4
wilderness! So last weekend we packed a tent and lots of

_____ and we went on a one-day "practice trip." We
          5
learned an important lesson—camping is hard work! Maybe the beach
is a better idea!

B. Understand the meaning of the words and phrases from context. Look back at the article on page 85. Choose words from the box with a similar meaning.

| a. be away from other people | b. expensive | c. not a beginner |

	Words in the text	Similar meaning	Paragraph
1.	cost a lot		2
2.	experienced		4
3.	go off alone		4

A. Take this quiz about your own study habits. Put an X under Yes or No. Discuss your answers with a partner.

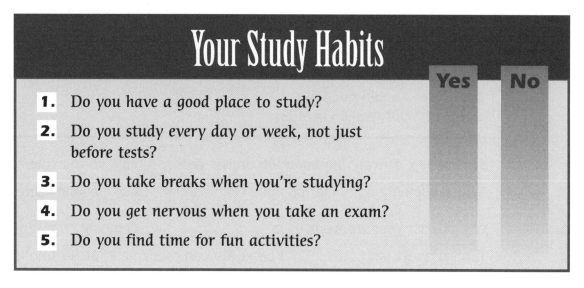

Your Study Habits

		Yes	No
1.	Do you have a good place to study?		
2.	Do you study every day or week, not just before tests?		
3.	Do you take breaks when you're studying?		
4.	Do you get nervous when you take an exam?		
5.	Do you find time for fun activities?		

B. Which of these phrases do you know? Put an X next to them. Ask your classmates about the other phrases, or look them up in a dictionary.

____ study habits   ____ make a schedule

____ study break   ____ review (for an exam)

____ take an exam   ____ take notes

C. Work in small groups. Put the phrases from B into the categories below. Some phrases can go in *more than one* category. Think of other words and phrases for the categories and add them to the chart. Compare your list with the other groups.

Classes	Homework	Studying for exams

9 WORDS YOU NEED

Guess which word is best for the sentences. Compare your answers with a partner.

1. My counselor gave me a good ____: always arrive a little early to class to get the best seat.

   a. test   b. tip   c. break

2. There are many ____ for taking good notes in class. Some people use different colors. Some people use spaces and indents. Some people record the lesson on a tape recorder.

   a. techniques   b. answers   c. results

3. Before an exam, she feels very nervous and worried. She feels ____ about exams.

   a. anxious   b. lucky   c. silly

4. He studies for a long time every day, but he ____ every hour.

   a. learns a technique   b. is on his own   c. takes a break

5. You shouldn't ____ the night before a test. It's better to study a little every day.

   a. review   b. take notes   c. cram

10 USE YOUR READING SKILLS

A. Preview the brochure on page 90 and make predictions. Answer the questions.

1. What is the topic of the text? _____

2. What will the brochure discuss? Mark your predictions with an X.

   ____ a. study habits
   ____ b. taking exams
   ____ c. deciding which classes to take
   ____ d. finding the right school
   ____ e. exercises to help you relax

B. Preview the comprehension questions (only the questions) on page 91. Predict the answers. As you read the article, underline the answers to the questions in the text.

This college brochure is for new students. It gives students tips on studying with more success.

Finding the Right Balance Between Studying and Fun

Welcome to college! We hope you have a lot of success in your studies, and we want to help you.

The most important thing for a student is good study habits. What are good study habits? The answer is different for each person. This information can help you to find *your* answer.

Which Study Habits Are Best for You?
Think about your study habits. Which work well for you, and which do you want to change? Here are some questions to ask yourself:

When do I study best?
Most people study better during the day, but some people study better at night.

How often do I take study breaks?
Breaks help people relax and focus. There are many relaxation techniques. When your body feels tense,[1] try this relaxation exercise.

Relaxation technique

Where do I study best?
Many people study best alone in a quiet place, but others study better with music on or with other people near them.

What balance do I have between studies and fun?
Does this balance work well for you? Some fun helps you to study better. Too much fun can be dangerous!

Tips for Studying for Exams
Studying for exams can make you feel anxious—nervous and worried. Here are some helpful tips to keep in mind:[2]

Don't cram!
You can't study everything the night before the test. A much better technique is to study a little every day.

Focus on important topics
Most teachers give study guides or review questions to their students before a test. Focus on that material.

Fight negative feelings
It's normal to feel anxious before a test. Try these techniques to help you relax:

Visualization: In your mind, get a picture of the day of the exam. In this picture, you are at your desk. You are taking the test, and you are doing well.
Self-talk: When you feel anxious, stop and say, "I know the material. I can do well." Positive self-talk can help you feel confident.

Studying and taking tests can be easier when you have good study habits. Try all these techniques then choose the right ones for you. Remember to balance your studies with relaxation and fun activities. Good luck!

[1] **tense:** not relaxed; stiff
[2] **keep in mind:** always remember

12 UNDERSTAND THE READING

A. Circle the correct answer.

1. What are good study habits for college students?

    a. Always study with friends.
    b. Never study with music on.
    c. They are different for each student.

2. What question should you ask yourself about your study habits?

    a. When do I study best?
    b. Why do I need to study?
    c. Which classes should I study for?

3. How can study breaks help you?

    a. They can help you to remember information.
    b. They can help you get exercise.
    c. They can help you relax.

4. When you study for an exam, how can you fight negative feelings?

    a. Cram for the exam.
    b. Use visualization.
    c. Don't review.

5. When should you move your shoulders in a circle?

    a. when you need to relax
    b. when you cram for an exam
    c. when you find time for fun activities

B. Think about your study habits. Which habits are good? Which habits do you want to change? In your notebook, write down three of these habits. With a partner, discuss them. Then write your answers.

Example: *I start studying after dinner.* ➝ *I want to start studying in the afternoon.*

13 WORK WITH THE VOCABULARY

Match the words and their descriptions.

_d_ **1.** anxious	a.	Marion wants to remember material, so she writes it down. This is her way to review.
___ **2.** cram	b.	Takeshi is studying, but he stops every hour for a few minutes.
___ **3.** take a break	c.	Shawna didn't study much this semester. She has to study all night for the test tomorrow morning.
___ **4.** a technique	d.	In exams, Martina feels nervous and worried and her body gets tense.

14

GET READY TO READ AND SHARE

Work with a partner. Look at the picture and read the situation. Discuss the questions. Then share your answers with your classmates.

Jessica works in an office. She's good at her job, but it doesn't interest her. She likes to be outside, to work with people, and to be active. Jessica wants to change jobs to balance her work life and her interests. Which job is best for Jessica? Why?

15

USE YOUR READING SKILLS

A. You are going to read one part of a magazine article about finding the right balance in work. Read the beginning of the article below. Then answer the questions.

Balancing Work and Interests
WHICH JOB IS RIGHT FOR YOU?

Do you need to find a better balance between your work life and your interests? You are not alone. Many people feel this way. Sometimes, finding a good balance means making a change in your job or your life, or both! The people in these stories changed their lives to find that perfect balance between work and interests.

1. Is it unusual for people to want a better balance between their work lives and their interests?

2. What kinds of changes do people sometimes make to find that balance?

B. First, preview Part A of the article and the Focus Questions on page 93. Second, preview Part B of the article and the Focus Questions on page 94. Then answer the questions below.

1. When Octavia changed her life, what did she do?

2. When Alayne and Steve changed their lives, what did they do?

Now choose one part of the article to read. Read Part A on page 93 <u>or</u> Part B on page 94.

Two Years in Africa

Volunteering in Africa

Octavia was a physics[1] student at a college in Texas. She liked physics and wanted to use her skills, but physicists[2] usually work on computers in offices. Octavia wasn't ready to sit at a desk all day every day. She was young and full of energy. After graduation, she wanted to use her skills, but she also wanted adventure.[3]

One day, there was a sign in the Student Center for the Peace Corps. The Peace Corps is a United States government organization. It sends volunteers to other countries to help people in different ways. Peace Corps volunteers teach, help farmers, and train people to use computers. Octavia went to a meeting to learn more about it. The day after graduation, she joined the Peace Corps!

Octavia went to Niger, in Africa. She taught physics in a high school. She also helped repair[4] buildings in the town. She even helped farmers build better farm equipment. Octavia used her physics skills in very interesting ways. She worked hard, but she also visited beautiful places and met wonderful people.

After two years in Niger, Octavia was an experienced physicist. She returned to the United States and found a job with a small company. Her company makes products to help communities around the world. Octavia works in an office, but she also travels a lot. Octavia found the perfect balance between her work and her interests.

[1] **physics:** the science of natural forces like light, sound, and weight
[2] **physicist:** an expert in physics
[3] **adventure:** excitement and unusual activities
[4] **repair:** to make an old or damaged thing useful again

Who can answer these questions about Part A with you? Find a partner. Answer the questions.

Focus Questions
1. Why didn't Octavia want to get a job as a physicist?
2. How did she use physics in Niger?
3. What does she do now?

The Rolling Dog Ranch Animal Sanctuary

Working with animals

Alayne and Steve both loved nature and animals, but they worked long hours in an office. They lived in Seattle, Washington, and worked for a large company. Their jobs were OK and they earned a lot of money, but they didn't feel satisfied.[1] They needed to make money, but they also wanted to work with animals.

One summer, Alayne and Steve went on a hiking vacation in Montana. There was an ad there: Land For Sale. They decided to buy the land and live on it when they retired.[2] They planned to start a sanctuary[3] for animals. Back in Seattle, Alayne and Steve thought about their land and their plan. They asked themselves, "Why wait?" They decided to go to Montana that same year!

Soon Alayne and Steve were in Montana—with dogs, cats, chickens, sheep, cows, donkeys, horses, and pigs. They called their home *The Rolling Dog Animal Sanctuary*. The animals at the sanctuary were old and sick. Some of them were disabled[4] in some way—for example, they weren't able to see, hear, or walk. Alayne and Steve cared for these animals, and they were safe and happy.

Alayne and Steve loved *The Rolling Dog Animal Sanctuary*. They earned less money, but they worked with animals. Their lives finally had the right balance, and they felt satisfied.

---

[1] **satisfied:** the feeling of having enough of something
[2] **retire:** to stop working, usually because of age
[3] **sanctuary:** safe place
[4] **disabled:** not able to use a part of the body well

Who can answer these questions about Part B with you? Find a partner. Answer the questions.

Focus Questions

1. How did Alayne and Steve feel about their jobs in Seattle?

2. What do they do at *The Rolling Dog Animal Sanctuary*?

3. How do they feel now? Why?

Organize Your Thoughts

Work with your partner. Complete the chart with information from your story.

Title of the story: ————————————————————————————

1. Who is the story about?

2. What was the situation at the beginning of the story?

3. What did she/they do about the situation?

4. What was the situation at the end of the story?

5. What kind of balance did she/they find?

Share Your Information

Who can tell you about the other story? Find another pair of classmates.

1. With your partner, tell the other pair of students about your story. Use the chart above.

2. Add some other details from your story.

Share Your Ideas

Discuss these questions with your partner and the other pair of students. Then share your answers with your classmates.

1. Do people have to change jobs to find a good balance in life?

2. What other kinds of changes can people make to find a good balance?

A. **Read these questions. Then read one student's answers.**

   1. Did you, a friend, or a family member do something to get a better balance in life? Who?

   2. What was the situation before?

   3. What did this person do to change it?

   4. What was the result?

> I am a quiet person. In the past, I never talked much at parties. I stayed home a lot, but I wanted to go out and have fun. I wanted more friends, but I was afraid to talk to people. Then I went to an acting class. This was a big challenge for me, but I decided to do it. I was very anxious in the beginning, but the class was fun and I found new friends. Now, I am much more comfortable with people. Sometimes I still stay home, but I also go out with my friends a lot. My life has a good balance now, and I'm happy.

B. **In a small group, discuss the questions.**

   1. How was this student's life not in balance?

   2. What did he do about it?

   3. In what ways is his life more balanced now?

C. **Now write your own paragraph. Answer the questions in A. Then add some details. You can use the student's paragraph as a model.**

Unit 7

That's Entertainment!

In this unit, you are going to:

● read about entertainment in the U.S.
● learn how to ask questions while you read

WHAT DO YOU KNOW ABOUT ENTERTAINMENT IN THE U.S.?

A. Look at this page from a newspaper. Which activities interest you? Which activities don't interest you? Discuss your answers with a partner.

EntertainmentNews

Activities Around Town This Weekend

Film
Classic Film Festival, Fri.-Sun. *See the Movie Reviews section for a complete listing.*

Sports
High School Football: Come to Springer Field and cheer for the Tigers! Friday, 8 p.m. $10 at the gate. (Also broadcast on Channel 73)

City League Soccer: Game on Sunday, noon, Simms Field. Want to play? $5 to join, come to practice Sat., 9 a.m.

Music
The Angry Puppy Band: Baxter Ballroom, Friday, 9 p.m. Tickets on sale at the box office. $30 in advance, $35 at the door.

Concert in the Park—*Oak Valley Band*: Mariposa Park, Saturday, 2 p.m. Free.

Theater
The Three Sisters: Westbury Community Theater, Saturday, 8 p.m. $12 at the door.

B. Think about these questions. Discuss your answers with your classmates.

1. What do you often do for entertainment when you are by yourself? What do you do with family and friends?

2. What is your favorite type of entertainment? Why?

1   GET READY TO READ ABOUT: Watching Television

A. Take this quiz. Guess the answers.

TV Viewing Habits in the United States

1. How many homes have at least one TV?	a. 50%	b. 78%	c. 99%
2. How many 8–12-year-olds have TVs in their rooms?	a. 21%	b. 46%	c. 65%
3. How many hours a day do 8–17-year-olds watch TV?	a. 2	b. 3	c. 5
4. How many hours a day do adults watch TV?	a. 1–2	b. 3–4	c. 5–6

B. Which of these words and phrases about TV do you know? Put an X next to
these words. Ask your classmates about the other words, or look them up in
a dictionary. Then add two words.

____ TV set   ____ TV station

____ TV program (TV show)   ____ remote control

____ commercial   _____

____ TV viewers   _____

2   BUILD YOUR READING SKILLS: Asking Questions While You Read

Introduction

A. Look at the cartoon. What is the woman asking herself? Why?

B. How can asking questions about a text help you understand it?

> **Asking questions while you read** helps you make predictions. Read one part of the text. Then ask yourself: *What did I learn? What will the next part be about?*

Practice Asking Questions While You Read

A. Read the first paragraph. Make a prediction about the next part. Circle your answer. Then read the next part and check your answer.

The Problems with Television

Educational television programs like Sesame Street are very good for children. They help young children learn. Television can also have a bad influence on children. This paper discusses some of the problems with TV for children.

What will the next part discuss?
  a. a bad children's program on TV
  b. a bad thing about TV for children

Children need to be active. They need to play outside and spend time with other children. Some children spend many hours in front of the TV and don't get enough exercise. This can cause children to gain weight and become fat. Childhood obesity, or very high weight, is increasing in the United States. TV is part of this problem.

B. What might the next part of the text in A be about? Discuss your predictions with your classmates.

Read the sentences. Guess the meaning of the underlined words. Circle the words with a similar meaning. Check your answers after you read the article on page 134.

1. Experts have many <u>concerns</u> about TV. For example, when children watch too much TV, they don't get enough exercise.

   a. worries
   b. studies
   c. activities

2. One of the harmful <u>effects</u> of TV is childhood obesity. Children don't play enough, and they gain weight.

   a. reasons
   b. results
   c. decisions

3. Some children don't like to watch TV, but the <u>average</u> child watches TV a lot.

   a. typical
   b. young
   c. teenage

4. Many TV programs show too much <u>violence</u>. These programs can give children wrong ideas about behavior.

   a. guns, fighting, and death
   b. comfort, challenge, and risk
   c. tips, techniques, and information

5. The people on TV shows usually have a lot of money. In <u>reality</u>, most people don't have a lot of money.

   a. real life
   b. life on television
   c. childhood

4 **USE YOUR READING SKILLS**

A. **Preview the article on pages 101–102 and make predictions. Answer the questions.**

   1. What is the topic of this article? _____

   2. Under which heading of the article will you find this information?

      a. Many people watch TV. <u>Surveys on TV Viewing Habits</u>

      b. TV can give us a lot of useful information. _____

      c. TV has many bad programs for children. _____

B. **Read the article on page 101. As you finish each part, make a prediction about the next part. Then read the next part and check your prediction.**

TV is an important part of life in the U.S., but is this good or bad? This article from a popular news magazine looks at the effects of television.

The Effects of Television: *Negative or Positive?*

Television is the most popular type of entertainment in the United States. Because TV is so popular, it is important to learn about TV viewing habits and to understand the effects of TV on people's lives.

1. What will the next part discuss?
a. other popular types of entertainment
b. facts about TV viewing habits

Surveys on TV Viewing Habits

Information from surveys about TV viewing habits in the United States is interesting. Almost every home has a TV set; many homes have several. Some children watch many hours of TV every day, but the average child watches about 3 hours a day. The average adult watches even more. What is the result of all this TV viewing? Some scientists are studying this, and they have real concerns about it.

2. What will the next part discuss?
a. opinions about TV programs
b. concerns about TV viewing

TV Viewing in the United States

- Homes with one or more TVs: **99%**
- Homes with three or more TVs: **66%**
- 8–12-year-olds with a TV in their room: **46%**
- 13–17-year-olds with a TV in their room: **56%**
- Average hours of TV viewing for children: 3 a day (20 a week)
- Average hours of TV viewing for adults: 3–4 a day (25 a week)

Source: Center for Media Literacy

The Negative Effects of TV

The biggest concern for scientists is time. American spend many hours a day in front of the TV. When people watch too much TV, they don't have balanced lives. They don't exercise, read, or spend enough time with friends and family.

Another concern is violence. Many people don't want guns, fighting, and death in their living rooms. In their opinion, violence on TV gives children wrong ideas. In reality, violence is not acceptable[1] in most situations, but TV makes it seem acceptable and normal. This can lead to behavior problems at school.

Of course, children do not have to watch programs with violence in them. There are many other options.[2] TV has many interesting and educational programs for children and adults.

3. What will the next part discuss?
a. some good things about TV
b. more concerns about TV

[1]**acceptable:** allowed, good for a situation
[2]**option:** choice

The Positive Effects of TV

Television can have positive effects on people's lives. It can be informative and educational. With so many TV channels, people can get lots of information about many topics. On TV, people learn about other cultures, other places, and other times in history. It gives viewers a bigger and better understanding of people and ideas.

TV also provides relaxation and entertainment for very little money. Relaxation and entertainment are important for health and happiness.

Television offers people many entertainment and information options. But, people must make their own decisions about the types of entertainment and information on their TVs. Their choices can have both positive and negative effects on themselves and their children. When people make good choices about television viewing, the positive effects will certainly be greater than the negative effects.

6 UNDERSTAND THE READING

A. **Complete the chart with words from the box.**

a. educational	b. entertaining	c. informative	d. relaxing	e. unhealthy

Example	Effect
1. Their kids watch TV shows with a lot of violence. Now, their behavior in school is not good.	TV can be _e_
2. Danilo had a long, difficult day at work. Now he's home and can watch some TV.	TV can be ____
3. Tonight's program is really funny. The whole family is laughing.	TV can be ____
4. Yesterday, Paul watched a show on Cuban cooking. Now he's cooking some Cuban food.	TV can be ____
5. My husband and I want to travel to Egypt. We watched a show about Egypt last night, and it answered a lot of our questions.	TV can be ____

B. **Look back at the quiz on page 98. Answer the questions again using the information from the article.**

C. **Think about the information in the article and your own TV viewing habits. Then work in a small group and answer the questions.**

1. Do Americans watch too much TV? Why or why not?

2. About how many hours a day do you watch TV? Is that too much?

3. What are some positive and negative effects of TV in your life?

7 WORK WITH THE VOCABULARY

A. Look at the table of contents from a magazine for parents. Complete the titles of the articles with words from the box. The descriptions of the articles can help you.

| a. average | b. concerns | c. effect | d. reality | e. violence |

Good Parents Magazine

This month's topic: Some ___ About Children and ......
Television Today
Parents today worry about television. Do experts also worry? We find out.

Page 3   Does the ___ Child Watch Too Much Television?
Does the typical child spend too much time in front of the TV?
We compare school kids across the United States and talk to experts.

Page 10   Does ___ on TV Have a Negative ___ on Children's Behavior?
People on TV hurt each other. Kids see this. What's the result? Psychologists give their opinions.

Page 21   TV Life and ___: Are Children Getting a Wrong Idea about Real Life from TV?
We ask kids for their ideas about money, homes, and jobs—are they the same on TV as in real life?

B. Complete the chart with the missing adjectives and nouns. Look back at the article on pages 101–102 to find the correct forms.

Noun	Adjective	Paragraph
1. entertainment	entertaining	1
2. balance		3
3.	real	4
4. education		6
5. information		6

C. Choose two of the missing words from B. Write a sentence for each one. Then share your sentences with your classmates.

A. Which activities do you enjoy? Mark your answers with a tick mark (|). Then work in a small group and survey the other students. Record all the responses with tick marks (卌). Share your results with the class.

Do you enjoy . . .	Yes	No
1. playing sports		
2. going dancing		
3. doing arts and crafts		
4. going hiking and camping		
5. going to the movies		
6. going to sports events		

B. Match the words to the people and things in the picture. Guess the answers. Check your answers after you read the article on pages 105–106.

1. band ____   2. contest ____   3. crops ____   4. farmer ____

9 WORDS YOU NEED

Read the definitions. Then complete the sentences with the correct definition.

    a. boring   not interesting

    b. event   any planned, special thing, like a football game or a play

    c. opportunity   a special chance to do something

    d. lose   to not win

1. In high school, he had the ____ to sing in a big contest. He won first prize!

2. The fair is opening next week! It's a big ____ in our town.

3. I like to go to the football games at the high school. Sometimes they win and sometimes they ____, but it's always a fun evening.

4. She likes to play sports and watch games. For her, movies and theater are not interesting. They are ____.

10 USE YOUR READING SKILLS

A. Preview the article below and make predictions. Answer the questions.

    1. What is the topic of this article? _____

    2. What kinds of entertainment does the article discuss? _____

    _____

B. Read the article below. As you finish each part, read the questions and circle a prediction. Then read the next part and check your prediction.

11 READ

In this tourism magazine, writer Annie Srisai remembers her life in a small town and discusses her favorite activities.

Big Fun in a Small Town

I was born in a small town, but now I live in a city. My friends here sometimes ask me: Is life in a small town boring? I always answer, No! In a small town, there are many entertaining activities. People do these activities together, and that makes the community stronger. A good example of this is high school football.

1. What will the next section discuss?
    a. high school football as entertainment
    b. stories of high school football players

Our high school football team plays every Friday night in the fall. The whole town comes to the football field—not just the students and their families, but everyone. The band and the cheerleaders help people cheer on[1] the team. Winning is important, but even when the home team loses, the game is an opportunity to talk to friends and have fun together.

High school football games happen every week, but another fun activity, the county fair, only happens once a year.

2. What will the next section discuss?
   a. activities at the county fair
   b. the dates and times of the county fair

The big event of the summer in my community is the county fair. In the past, county fairs were places for farmers to show and sell their crops and animals. Today, they are much more! At today's county fairs you can still find prize-winning animals and crops, but you can also find crafts, lots of food, rides, games, and many exciting contests.

County fairs are like their communities. When communities change, county fairs change. County fairs across the United States now have even more kinds of crafts and foods because of the immigrants in their communities. For example, in my community, there are now a lot of people from Thailand. At the fair, they perform[2] beautiful Thai dances. People love to watch the dances. In fact, people in our community enjoy many types of theater and shows.

3. What will the next section discuss?
   a. theater and shows in a small town
   b. immigrant groups in small towns

The community theater in my town is very popular. My whole family worked in the community theater, and my parents still work there. The community theater gives people in the town the opportunity to be actors and to entertain lots of people in the community. Sometimes, actors or musicians from other towns come to the theater. They perform for one or two nights, and almost everybody goes to see them.

Some people say: Life in a small town is too boring. Well, those people never visited MY town. My mind is full of wonderful memories[3]—memories of high school football games, county fairs, theater, and memories of being part of a community.

[1] **cheer on:** shout and show support for
[2] **perform:** to do a show for other people
[3] **memories:** things that you remember

12 UNDERSTAND THE READING

A. Circle the correct answer.

1. The writer thinks activities in small towns ____ .

    a. are not very interesting
    b. give people a feeling of community
    c. are very similar to activities in cities

2. High school football games are important because ____ .

    a. people in the community can get together, talk, and have fun
    b. players can cheer on the band and cheerleaders
    c. schools use the money for books and other supplies

3. County fairs today are different from early county fairs because ____ .

    a. fairs today have farm products
    b. fairs today have rides and games
    c. fairs today are in cities

4. Community theater is ____ .

    a. a place for high school football games
    b. a place for farmers to sell their crops
    c. a place for people in the town to be actors for fun

B. Work in a small group. Discuss these questions.

1. Which has more entertaining activities—a small town or big city?

2. Which has a greater feeling of community—a small town or big city?

3. Which do you prefer—small towns or big cities? Why?

13 WORK WITH THE VOCABULARY

Circle the correct word in each sentence. Check your answers with a partner.

1. This play is very (boring/entertaining). I'm not interested in it at all. Let's leave.

2. July 4th is a big (event/opportunity) is our town. We plan many special activities and have fun contests for the kids.

3. Sammi is a very good dancer, but in our small town she doesn't have many (opportunities/prizes) to perform. She's moving to the city.

4. My father is always in the hot dog eating contest. Every year, he tries to win, but he always (wins/loses).

14 GET READY TO READ AND SHARE

Read the movie advertisement. Guess the meaning of the underlined words. Discuss your answers with your classmates.

15 USE YOUR READING SKILLS

A. You are going to read a review for the movie *Jaws*. First, read the summary of the movie from a movie Web site below. Then answer the questions.

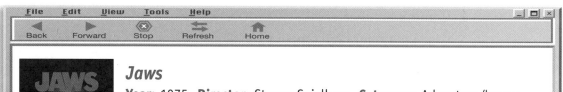

File   Edit   View   Tools   Help

Back   Forward   Stop   Refresh   Home

Jaws

Year: 1975 **Director:** Steven Spielberg **Category:** Adventure/horror

Main characters: Actor Roy Scheider, as Police Chief Martin Brody
Actor Robert Shaw, as boat captain Quint
Actor Richard Dreyfuss, as shark expert Matt Hooper

The Story: A shark attacks and kills a teenage girl near the town of Amity. The Amity Police Chief wants to close the beach, but the people in the town government want to keep the beach open. Many tourists come to Amity for vacation every summer, and the town doesn't want them to leave. The beach stays open, and the shark kills again. Now the town must do something. They hire Quint to kill the shark. Quint, Brody, and a shark expert, Hooper, go out in Quint's boat to find the shark. Can they save the town of Amity from the killer shark?

1. Why doesn't Amity want to close its beach?

2. Who is Quint? What did the town hire him to do?

B. Preview Review A and Review B on pages 109 and 110. For each review, look at the reviewer line, summary line, and the focus questions. Then answer these questions.

1. What is Victor's opinion of Jaws?   a. positive   b. negative
2. What is Erik's opinion of Jaws?   a. positive   b. negative

Now choose one review to read. Read Review A on page 109 _or_ Review B on page 110.

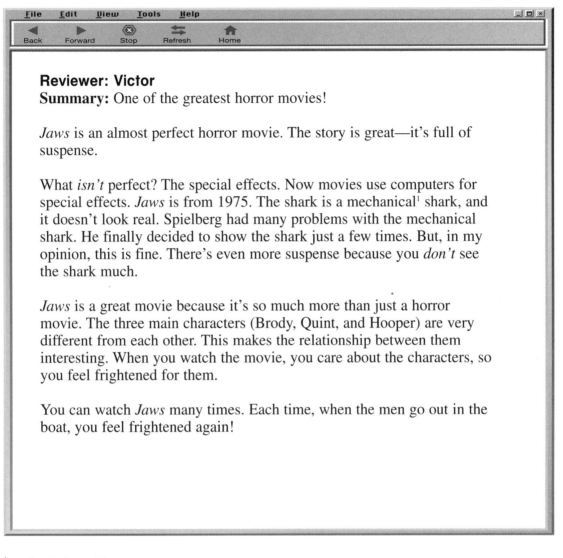

Reviewer: Victor
Summary: One of the greatest horror movies!

Jaws is an almost perfect horror movie. The story is great—it's full of suspense.

What *isn't* perfect? The special effects. Now movies use computers for special effects. *Jaws* is from 1975. The shark is a mechanical[1] shark, and it doesn't look real. Spielberg had many problems with the mechanical shark. He finally decided to show the shark just a few times. But, in my opinion, this is fine. There's even more suspense because you *don't* see the shark much.

Jaws is a great movie because it's so much more than just a horror movie. The three main characters (Brody, Quint, and Hooper) are very different from each other. This makes the relationship between them interesting. When you watch the movie, you care about the characters, so you feel frightened for them.

You can watch *Jaws* many times. Each time, when the men go out in the boat, you feel frightened again!

[1] **mechanical:** machine

Who can answer these questions about Review A with you? Find a partner. Answer the questions.

Focus Questions
1. What isn't perfect about Jaws? Why?
2. What makes Jaws a suspenseful movie?
3. What makes Jaws a great horror movie?

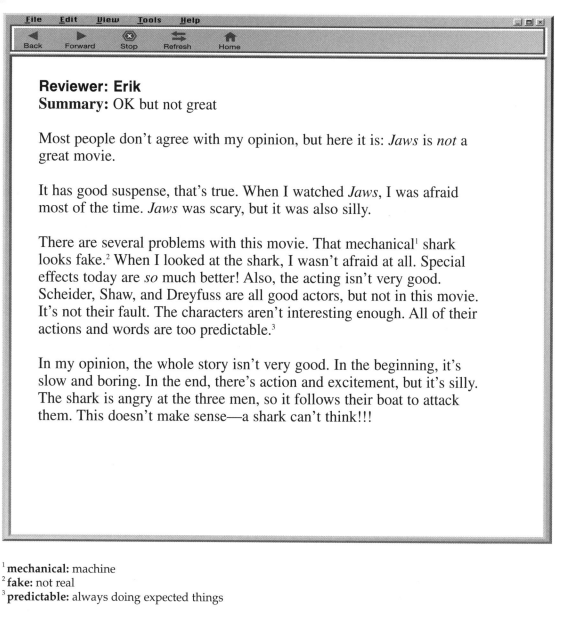

Reviewer: Erik
Summary: OK but not great

Most people don't agree with my opinion, but here it is: *Jaws* is *not* a great movie.

It has good suspense, that's true. When I watched *Jaws*, I was afraid most of the time. *Jaws* was scary, but it was also silly.

There are several problems with this movie. That mechanical[1] shark looks fake.[2] When I looked at the shark, I wasn't afraid at all. Special effects today are *so* much better! Also, the acting isn't very good. Scheider, Shaw, and Dreyfuss are all good actors, but not in this movie. It's not their fault. The characters aren't interesting enough. All of their actions and words are too predictable.[3]

In my opinion, the whole story isn't very good. In the beginning, it's slow and boring. In the end, there's action and excitement, but it's silly. The shark is angry at the three men, so it follows their boat to attack them. This doesn't make sense—a shark can't think!!!

[1] **mechanical:** machine
[2] **fake:** not real
[3] **predictable:** always doing expected things

Who can answer these questions about Review B with you? Find a partner. Answer the questions.

Focus Questions

1. What is good about Jaws?

2. What problems does Jaws have?

3. What doesn't make sense about the movie?

17 THINK AND SHARE

Organize Your Thoughts

Work with your partner. Put an X in the correct column of the chart for your review.

Review of *Jaws*	Good	Bad
1. The movie in general		
2. The suspense		
3. The story		
4. The special effects		
5. The characters and the acting		

Share Your Information

Who can tell you about the other review? Find another pair of classmates.

1. With your partner, share your answers from the chart above with the other pair of students.

2. Explain the reviewer's reasons for each point. Do the reviewers agree on any points?

Share Your Ideas

Discuss these questions with your partner and the other pair of students. Then share your answers with the class.

1. Do you want to see *Jaws*, for the first time or again? Why or why not?

2. Why do people like suspenseful movies? What are some examples of each type?

3. Are movies better with special effects or without them? Why?

18 REFLECT ON: Entertainment

A. Read these questions. Then read one student's review.

1. What movie did you see recently? Where did you see it?

2. What is the story?

3. Did you like the movie? Why or Why not?

4. What is good about the movie? What is bad about it?

> I watched the movie Alexander last week. I watched it at home. It is about a famous leader in history. I like history, so I wanted to see it. It was not good. The movie story was very different from the real story of Alexander the Great. The other characters were also very different from history, but the acting was OK. The special effects were good. The fighting looked real. This is a good action movie, but it is NOT a good history movie.

B. In a small group, discuss these questions.

1. Did the student like the movie? Why or why not?

2. What was good about it? What was not good?

C. Now write your own review. Answer the questions in A. Then add some details. You can use the student's review as a model.

Unit 8

The Comforts of Home

In this unit, you are going to:

● read about homes in the U.S.
● learn how to scan a text for specific information

WHAT DO YOU KNOW ABOUT HOMES IN THE UNITED STATES?

A. Work with a partner. Look at the ad and the floor plan for an apartment. What do the abbreviations in the ad stand for? Is this a good apartment for you? Why or why not?

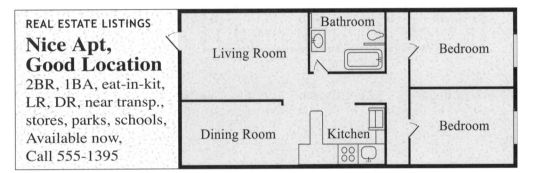

REAL ESTATE LISTINGS

Nice Apt, Good Location

2BR, 1BA, eat-in-kit, LR, DR, near transp., stores, parks, schools, Available now, Call 555-1395

B. Complete the survey. Mark one choice in each item with an X. Share your answers with your classmates.

Home Preferences Survey

I prefer to live in . . .

1.	____ an apartment.	____ a house.
2.	____ a quiet location.	____ a convenient location.
3.	____ a comfortable home.	____ a beautiful home.
4.	____ an area with lots of privacy.	____ a busy area.
5.	____ a modern home.	____ a traditional home.

A. Work with a partner. Find the words from the Word List in the puzzle and circle them. Then write the words in the correct categories below. Some words can go in more than one category. Add one word to each category.

S	H	O	W	E	R	T	J	C	R	I	K
S	L	U	N	B	T	A	A	R	X	Z	G
T	D	Y	L	O	U	B	C	O	U	C	H
I	R	E	W	I	V	L	R	B	L	L	M
R	E	F	R	I	G	E	R	A	T	O	R
O	S	A	U	D	W	H	N	G	B	S	V
H	S	E	G	O	E	J	T	D	D	E	T
S	E	C	O	O	T	O	I	L	E	T	D
A	R	P	N	R	W	I	N	D	O	W	P
F	O	C	E	I	L	I	N	G	H	U	I

Word List

~~bed~~	oven
ceiling	refrigerator
closet	rug
couch	shower
door	table
dresser	toilet
light	window

Living Room	Bedroom	Bathroom	Kitchen
	bed		

B. Think about homes in the year 2050. Use your imagination. Discuss your ideas with a partner. Then share your ideas with your classmates.

In 2050, homes will be very different from homes today. How will they be different?

Example: In 2050, robots will clean homes.

2 BUILD YOUR READING SKILLS: Scanning

Introduction

A. Look at the picture. How will this man find the most important information and also catch the bus?

B. How can you find specific information in any kind of text quickly?

Reading Skill

> **Scanning** means looking for specific information in a text. When you scan, you move your eyes quickly down the page to look for the information. To scan for dates, look for numbers. To scan for names of people or special places, look for capital letters.

Practice Scanning

A. Scan the paragraph for these numbers. Answer the questions.

1. What happened in 1867? _____

2. What happened in 1959? _____

B. Scan the paragraph for these names. Answer these questions.

1. What was Louis Sullivan's job? _____

2. Where is Fallingwater? _____

Frank Lloyd Wright designed some of the most famous buildings in the United States. He was a great architect. Wright was born in 1867. He first worked with architect Louis Sullivan in Chicago, Illinois. Then he started his own office in Oak Park, Illinois. He designed many famous homes and buildings. He also thought of many new ideas and architectural techniques. His work includes the house Fallingwater, in Pennsylvania, and the Guggenheim Museum, in New York City. Wright died in 1959. Students of architecture still study his ideas today.

3 WORDS YOU NEED

Read the paragraph. Then match the underlined words from the paragraph to the definitions below.

Most modern homes have many appliances. These appliances do many jobs for people and <u>simplify</u> life. They cook food, clean clothes, and <u>monitor</u> homes—a smoke alarm, for example, monitors smoke and the temperature of the air. Appliances are helpful, but many of them use a lot of energy. This is bad for the <u>environment</u>, or the natural world. Scientists are trying to create better <u>technology</u> for appliances— technology to help appliances use less electricity. Until the new technology is available, people should think about the way they use their appliances and try to use them less often.

1. _____ : science and ideas about how things work

2. _____ : to make something easier

3. _____ : to check and record information about something

4. _____ : the air, water, land, animals, and plants around us

4 USE YOUR READING SKILLS

A. Preview the article on page 117. Answer the questions.

1. What is the topic of this article? _____

2. What does this article have information about? _____

_____

B. Scan the article to answer these questions. Look for the numbers and capital letters.

1. What happened in 1957? _____

_____

2. What will happen by 2030? _____

_____

3. What does the abbreviation MIT stand for? _____

_____

4. Where does Kent Larson work? _____

_____

C. Read the article on page 117. After you finish each part, make a prediction about the next part. Then read the next part.

Architects and scientists are working together to plan the house of the future. This article in a science magazine is about their research and ideas.

The House of the Future

Have a salad

Architects in the past and today have the same question: What will the house of the future look like? In 1957, a group of architects showed their idea for "The House of the Future" at Disneyland. It was almost all plastic! Architects today don't want to guess about the future. They are using science to help make their predictions.

Research Today for Tomorrow's Homes

At MIT (the Massachusetts Institute of Technology), researchers built[1] *The PlaceLab*. It is a one-bedroom apartment. Volunteers live in The PlaceLab. Researchers watch the volunteers and study their behavior. This gives the researchers information about people's needs. It also gives them ideas for new technology. They call their ideas *smart house technology*.

Smart House Technology

Smart houses will use computer technology to control the home, to save energy, and to improve people's health. In a smart house, electronic sensors[2] will be in the floors, walls, ceilings, and windows. These sensors will send information to a central computer. The central computer will then help control the house. It will also monitor the people in the house and give advice. For example, when a person is over his or her ideal weight, the sensor in the floor will "feel" this. The computer will send a message to a cell phone or watch. The message will read, "You should have a light lunch today—maybe a salad." Smart houses will influence every part of people's daily lives.

Life in a Smart House

"Smart houses will help people in many different ways," says MIT architect Kent Larson. Parents will be able to monitor their children better. The house will know about a child's location and activities. Smart houses will also help seniors live independently.[3] The house will monitor their health and remind them to take medicine. Smart houses will also help the environment. When a room is empty, the computer will turn off the lights, close the curtains on the windows, and change the temperature to save energy. Some of these things are even possible today.

Most of the technology for smart houses—computers, cell phones, sensors—is already available.[4] We just need to put it all together. Architects want to start using smart house technology in new houses and apartment buildings. By 2030, researchers say, the "house of the future" will be just another normal house.

[1] **built:** the past tense of *build*
[2] **sensor:** a small electronic device for monitoring sound, light, temperature, etc.
[3] **independently:** without help
[4] **available:** ready to use

A. Each of these sentences about life in smart houses is incorrect. Cross out all the incorrect words and write the correct words. Look back at the article on page 117 to check your answers.

1. This article is about houses of the ~~past~~. *future*

2. The "House of the Future" in 1957 was almost all wood.

3. The PlaceLab at MIT is a two-bedroom apartment.

4. Smart houses use television technology to control the house.

5. Sensors will send people to a central computer.

6. Smart houses will help young people live alone.

B. Work in a small group. Discuss the questions. Write your answers in the correct category of the chart. Then share your answers with your classmates.

In a smart house, a central computer controls and monitors everything and everybody. What are some possible problems with this idea? What are some possible benefits?

Problems	Benefits
When there is no electricity, nothing works.	The house will turn off the lights for you.

A. Choose the best example sentence for each word.

____ **1.** monitor   a. "Maybe my daughter is in her room."
               b. "I always know my daughter's location."
               c. "My daughter likes to play in her room."

____ **2.** environment   a. "Saving energy is good for the Earth."
               b. "Architecture has a big influence on people."
               c. "Cell phones can help us communicate better."

____ **3.** simplify   a. "Computer technology is already available."
               b. "A computer makes my work easier."
               c. "Computers use a lot of energy."

____ **4.** technology   a. "This area has many trees and a lake."
               b. "New appliances need sensors and computer parts."
               c. "My apartment has a two bedrooms and one bathroom."

B. Complete the sentences with the correct verb phrase. Circle your answers. Look back at the article on page 117 to help you.

1. What will the house of the future ____ ? Probably, it will be very different from today's houses.

     a. look at   b. look for   c. look like

2. When a room is empty, a smart house will ____ the light.

     a. turn on   b. turn around   c. turn off

3. Researchers at MIT want to ____ computer technology and architecture ____ to create smart houses.

     a. put . . . together   b. put . . . behind   c. put . . . down

C. Look back at paragraph 3 of the article on page 117. Find the phrase "light lunch." Use the context to help you guess the definition. Check your answer with a partner.

A. Work with a partner. Look at these American inventions for the home. Read their names below. Match the name of each invention with the correct picture. Compare your answers with your classmates.

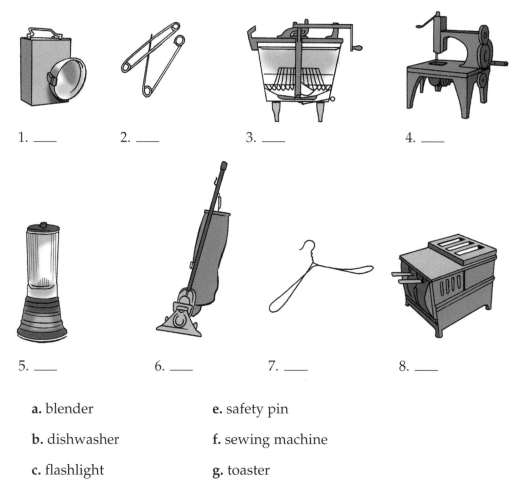

1. ___   2. ___   3. ___   4. ___

5. ___   6. ___   7. ___   8. ___

a. blender   **e.** safety pin

b. dishwasher   **f.** sewing machine

c. flashlight   **g.** toaster

d. hanger   **h.** vacuum cleaner

B. Quiz your partner on the names of the inventions above. Cover the names of the inventions with your hands. Take turns pointing to one picture and asking your partner, "What is it?" Continue until you can each correctly name all the inventions.

C. Work in a small group. Discuss the questions. Then share your answers with your classmates.

   1. Which three inventions from A above are the most useful? Why?

   2. Which three inventions from A above are the least useful? Why?

   3. Which of the inventions in A above do you use? Which don't you use?

9 WORDS YOU NEED

Complete the sentences with the words from the box. Use each word one time. Check your answers after you read the article on page 122.

| a. air conditioning | b. can opener | c. frozen dinner | d. frozen food |

1. A lot of food comes in metal cans. To get the food out, people need to use a ____ .

2. Some people buy food from the freezer at the supermarket. When they want to eat it, they take it out of their freezer at home and cook it. This kind of food is called ____ .

3. Many people don't like to cook. They buy cooked meals from the freezer at the supermarket. When they want to eat one, they only have to heat it, not cook it. This kind of meal is called a ____ .

4. In very hot areas of the country, people need to cool the temperature in the house. They use ____ .

10 USE YOUR READING SKILLS

A. Preview the Web page on page 122. Answer the questions.

1. What is the topic of this Web page? _____

2. Which invention does it discuss first? _____

B. Scan the article to answer the questions.

1. What happened in 1858? _____

_____

2. Where did Clarence Birdseye visit? _____

_____

3. What did C. A. Swanson have? _____

_____

4. What did Willis Carrier invent in 1902? _____

_____

This Web page tells the story of some helpful U.S. inventions for the home.

INVENTIONS All Around Us

Canned food and the can opener
Frozen food
Frozen dinners
Air conditioning

Every invention has a story. These stories often have a lesson to teach, too. Here are the stories of some everyday household inventions.

Canned Food and the Can Opener—Get It Right!

Peter Durand invented canned food in 1813, but there was a problem. Durand didn't have a good way to open the cans. In 1858, Ezra Warner invented a can opener. It used a piece of metal to make a hole in the can. Then you pushed the sharp metal around the top of the can. It removed the top from the can, but it was difficult to use. Finally, in 1925, William Lyman added a wheel to the can opener. The sharp metal rolled around the top of the can and removed it easily. Finally, people were able to open cans without a lot of work. Canned food was soon popular.

Frozen Food—A Little Good Luck Can Help!

Clarence Birdseye had the chance to go on a trip to the Arctic.[1] When people there caught[2] fish, they put the fish in a container of ice to freeze[3] it quickly. When people cooked the fish later, it was still good! This gave Birdseye an idea. In 1926, Birdseye invented frozen food. People were able to store food in freezers for a long time.

Frozen Dinners—A Little Bad Luck Can Help, Too!

C. A. Swanson had 260 tons[4] of extra turkey meat and no place to put it. The turkey was not frozen. It was in refrigerated train cars, but the refrigerators only worked when the train moved. The turkey traveled around the country in the train cars while Swanson thought about the problem. Finally, an employee had an idea. "Don't sell the turkey," he said. "Sell a turkey dinner!" They cooked and sliced the turkey. Then they froze it in a metal tray with potatoes and vegetables. In 1953, the frozen dinner (or TV dinner) was born!

Can opener with wheel

Air Conditioning—One Solution for Two Problems!

Printing companies make books, so they use a lot of paper. Sometimes, changes in the weather can hurt the paper. In 1902, Willis Carrier invented air conditioning to control the temperature inside his printing company. This saved the paper. People soon realized other benefits of air conditioning. They started to air condition their homes and offices in the summer. Carrier's invention changed the country! Today, 80% of people in the United States use air conditioning in their homes and businesses.

---

[1] **Arctic:** the far north of the Earth
[2] **caught:** the past tense of *catch*
[3] **freeze:** to make something as cold or colder than ice
[4] **ton:** a measure of weight equal to 2,000 pounds

12 UNDERSTAND THE READING

A. Circle the correct answers.

1. When Peter Durand first invented cans, ___.

   a. they were quickly popular
   b. they were difficult to open
   c. they changed people's eating habits

2. The first can opener ___.

   a. was a lot of work to use
   b. rolled around the top of the can
   c. was very expensive

3. After his trip to the Arctic, Clarence Birdseye invented ___.

   a. frozen food
   b. TV dinners
   c. refrigerated trains

4. Before air conditioning, the temperature sometimes ___.

   a. hurt cooked and sliced turkey
   b. hurt printing paper
   c. hurt canned food

B. Work with a partner. Answer the questions. Scan the article on page 122 for help.

1. Why did William Lyman's can opener work so well?

2. What is another name for Swanson's frozen dinner? Why do you think it has that name?

13 WORK WITH THE VOCABULARY

Look at this word family. Use the context to help you complete the sentences with the correct form.

Verb (present tense)	Verb (past tense)	Noun	Adjective
a. freeze	b. froze	c. freezer	d. frozen

1. Birdseye invented ___ food, and people were able to store it for a long time.

2. Supermarkets store TV dinners in the ___.

3. They cooked and sliced the turkey, then they ___ it in a metal tray.

4. People in the Arctic put the fish in a container of ice to ___ it quickly.

14 GET READY TO READ AND SHARE ABOUT: Unusual Houses

A. Work with a partner. Answer the questions.

House A

House B

1. Which house is ordinary?

2. Which house is unusual? In what ways is it unusual?

B. Work in a small group. Look at this list of words. How many of the words do you know? Put an X next to these words, or look them up in a dictionary.

____ roof   ____ stone   ____ family room

____ grill (*n.*)   ____ deck   ____ hot tub

15 USE YOUR READING SKILLS

A. You are going to read one part of a magazine article about unusual homes. Read the introduction to the article below. Then answer the questions.

Home   TWO UNUSUAL HOMES

Most people are happy in ordinary houses and apartments. They don't even think about other possibilities. Some people get an idea about a different kind of home, and they work to make their idea a reality. This article is the story of two unusual homes and their owners.

1. What kind of home do most people like?

2. What kind of homes do the people in this article like?

B. Preview Part A and Part B of the magazine article on pages 125 and 126. Answer questions 1 and 2. Then scan the two parts for the answers to questions 3 and 4.

1. Why is the Stacys' house unusual?   3. When did the Stacys build their house?

2. Why is the Lines' house unusual?   4. When did the Lines build their house?

Now choose one part of the article to read. Read Part A on page 125 <u>or</u> Part B on page 126.

The Mother Goose House

One day George Stacy asked his wife, Ollie, to cook a goose. He then asked her to remove all the meat. He went with the skeleton[1] to an architect. George Stacy and the architect used it to design a goose house. How did George Stacy get this idea? Nobody knows. He didn't even like geese.

The Stacys built the Mother Goose House from stone. They built it in Hazard, Kentucky, but the stones were from many different places. They worked on the house from 1935 to 1940. It's a two-story house with three bedrooms, a bathroom, a kitchen, a living room, a dining room, and a family room. The rooms are not unusual, but in every other way the house is very unusual. The eight windows of the house are all shaped like goose eggs. One end of the roof has a 15-foot-tall goose's head, with blue headlights[2] from a car for eyes; the other end has a 10-foot-long tail. The house is round and has small trees around it, so it looks like a goose on a nest.[3]

It was difficult for the Stacys to build their house. They didn't have much money for it, but they continued to work on it together. Both George and Ollie Stacy are dead now, but you can drive through Hazard and still see their famous Mother Goose House.

[1] **skeleton:** the bones of a whole animal or person
[2] **headlights:** the two big, strong lights on the front of a car
[3] **nest:** place where birds live and lay eggs

Who can answer these questions about Part A with you? Find a partner. Answer the questions.

Focus Questions

1. What did George Stacy and the architect use to design the house?

2. Why did the Stacys build an unusual house?

3. What is unusual about the Stacys' house?

The Tree House

Will and Peggy Line started building the tree house just for fun. Then they had an idea—the tree house could be a good place for guests. On a piece of paper, they made[1] a plan for this guest treehouse.

The Lines built the tree house from 2001 to 2003 from many different kinds of wood. They did all the work themselves. The more they worked on the tree house, the more they liked it. Then they had a second idea—*they* could live in the tree house!

The Lines' tree house is in the town of Wadena, Minnesota. They built it 14 feet from the ground. It has two stories. There's a main floor with a living room, kitchen, and bathroom. Above that, there are rooms for sleeping. They also built a big deck with holes for the tree's branches.[2] On the deck, the Lines have a hot tub and a grill. The tree house has water and electricity. It's unusual, but it's a real house. The Lines' mailing address is unusual, too. Their address is just "The Tree House."

The Lines love everything about living in the tree house—listening to the rain on the roof, watching the trees in the wind, waking up with the sun, eating on the deck. They don't miss their old house. And they certainly don't get lonely.[3] Every day, people drive by, notice the tree house, and visit the Lines.

[1] **made:** past tense of *make*
[2] **branch:** parts of a tree, often with leaves
[3] **lonely:** unhappy because you are alone

Who can answer these questions about Part B with you? Find a partner. Answer the questions.

Focus Questions

1. Why did the Lines start to build a treehouse?
2. What was their first idea about the treehouse? What was their second idea?
3. What is unusual about the Lines' home?

Organize Your Thoughts

Work with your partner. First, answer the question in the middle. Then answer the other questions starting at the top with "Who?" Write some details for each of the questions on the extra lines. Finish the chart with "Decribe."

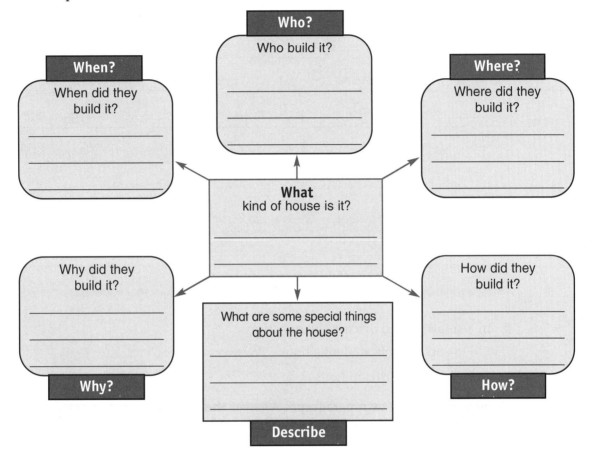

Share Your Information

Who can tell you about the other house? Find a pair of classmates. Then share your information.

1. With your partner, share your answers from the chart above with the other pair of students.

2. Give your opinion of the house in your part of the article.

Share Your Ideas

Discuss the questions with your partner and the other pair of students. Then share your answers with classmates.

Imagine this situation: You can live in one of these houses. Which one will you choose? Why?

18 REFLECT ON: The Home of Your Dreams

A. Read these questions. Then read one student's answers.

Imagine this situation: You can live in the home of your dreams.

1. What kind of home will you live in? How big will it be? Where will it be?

2. Will it be a "smart house"? Why or why not? What "smart" things will it do?

3. Will it be an unusual home? In what ways will be it unusual?

> I'll live in a house at the beach. My house will be small, but it will have an extra bedroom for guests. The walls in my house will have many colors. I don't want a smart house. I like to cook and clean. My house will have an unusual roof. The roof will open, like a window. I will see the stars when I go to sleep. I'll have a deck with a table outside. I will eat my meals and watch the ocean.

B. In a small group, discuss the questions.

1. Do you like this student's house? Why or why not?

2. What is your dream house?

C. Now write your own paragraph. Answer the questions in A. Then add some details. You can use the student's paragraph as a model.

Answer Key

Exercises for which answers vary are not included in the Answer Key.

Unit 1 Finding Happiness

1. GET READY TO READ ABOUT
(p. 2)

1. a 2. d 3. c 4. b

2. BUILD YOUR READING SKILLS

Practice Previewing (p. 3)

1. For Kids, Happiness Is a Soccer Game
2. Kids on a soccer team
3. a 4. a

3. WORDS YOU NEED (p. 4)

1. a 2. b 3. c 4. d 5. e

4. USE YOUR READING SKILLS
(p. 4)

1. b 2. a

6. UNDERSTAND THE READING

Exercise A (p. 6)

1. c 2. a 3. b 4. a 5. a

7. WORK WITH VOCABULARY

Exercise A (p. 7)

2. compare   4. happiness
3. research   5. wealthy
                 6. expert

8. GET READY TO READ ABOUT

Exercise A (p. 8)

1. d 2. b 3. a 4. e 5. c

9. WORDS YOU NEED (p. 9)

1. d 2. c 3. b 4. a

10. USE YOUR READING SKILLS
(p. 9)

1. c 2. a

12. UNDERSTAND THE READING

Exercise B (p. 11)

1. F 2. F 3. F 4. T 5. T

13. WORK WITH VOCABULARY

Exercise A (p.11)

1. positive attitude   3. advice
2. agree   4. gets to know

Exercise B (p. 11)

1. b 2. b

14. GET READY TO READ AND SHARE

Exercise A (p. 12)

1. f 2. a 3. c 4. e 5. d 6. b

15. USE YOUR READING SKILLS

Exercise A (p. 12)

1. two women who volunteer in their community
2. 65 million people

Exercise B (p. 12)

1. a 2. b

16. READ PART A

Focus Questions (p. 13)

1. seniors and their families
2. she goes on the bus with the seniors; she helps them feel comfortable; she helps them with their shopping; she spends time with them at the doctor's office
3. to help other people

16. READ PART B

Focus Questions (p. 14)

1. children in the Edgewood Court Apartments
2. she tutors children
3. it makes her feel good; she wants to help kids in her community

17. THINK AND SHARE
Organize Your Thoughts (p. 15)

Questionnaire Answers for A

1. Hap Johnson
2. She's in her 70s.
3. DARTS
4. It helps seniors and their families.
5. She goes with seniors on buses.
6. She can help other people and be active.

Questionnaire Answers for B

1. Tianna Bailey
2. She's in her 20s.
3. IMAGE
4. It helps kids in the Edgewood Court Apartments.
5. She helps kids with their homework.
6. The kids are doing better at school.

18. REFLECT ON: Happiness

Exercise B (p. 16)

1. the food in the cafeteria because it is usually bad; he can learn to cook and make his own food

Unit 2 It's Great to Communicate!

1. GET READY TO READ ABOUT

Exercise C (p. 18)

a, c

2. BUILD YOUR READING SKILLS

Practice Previewing and Making Predictions (p. 19)

1. a 2. b, c

3. WORDS YOU NEED (p. 20)

1. e 2. a 3. d 4. b 5. c

4. USE YOUR READING SKILLS

Exercise A (p. 20)

a

Exercise B (p. 20)

a, b, d, e

6. UNDERSTAND THE READING

Exercise A (p. 22)

1. b 2. c 3. b 4. b 5. c

7. WORK WITH VOCABULARY

Exercise A (p. 23)

1. show interest
2. make decisions, make rules
3. discuss problems
4. express feelings

Exercise B (p. 23)

communication
decision
explanation
discussion

9. WORDS YOU NEED (p. 25)

1. honest, kind
2. misunderstanding
3. avoid, solve

10. USE YOUR READING SKILLS
(p. 25)

1. c 2. b, e

12. UNDERSTAND THE READING

Exercise A (p. 27)

1. c 2. b 3. a 4. f

13. WORK WITH VOCABULARY
(p. 27)

1. interrupt   2. unkind
3. misunderstandings   4. avoid

14. GET READY TO READ AND SHARE (p. 28)

1. message   4. reply
2. post   5. screen name
3. subject

15. USE YOUR READING SKILLS

Exercise A (p. 29)

1. her friend is always with her boyfriend
2. he's not right for her friend

Exercise B (p. 29)

1. b   2. a

16. READ REPLY A

Focus Questions (p. 29)

1. she might feel hurt, angry, or unhappy; maybe her boyfriend is right for her
2. she spends a lot of time with her boyfriend; she doesn't see Ana Banana often

16. READ REPLY B

Focus Questions (p. 30)

1. they can help you think better
2. you're not being honest; your friendship will feel false

17. THINK AND SHARE

Organize Your Thoughts (p. 31)

Sentences for Reply A

Don't talk to her.

Maybe her boyfriend is right for her.

Maybe you are jealous.

Sentences for Reply B

Talk to her.

Your ideas can help her think better.

You need to be honest with her.

Sentences for Reply A and Reply B

Friends don't always agree.

You want your friend to be happy.

Unit 3 Success in the U.S.

1. GET READY TO READ ABOUT

Exercise A (p. 34)

1. in the past
2. young; poor

Exercise C (p. 34)

Positive	Negative
hard-working	dishonest
honest	lazy
kind	

2. BUILD YOUR READING SKILLS

Introduction

Exercise B (p. 35)

nouns

Practice Connecting Pronouns to Nouns (p. 35)

He/ Dick; them/ People; He/ Dick

He/ Mr. Greyson; his/ Mr. Greyson's; They/ shoes; his/ Dick's

3. WORDS YOU NEED (p. 36)

1. d   2. b   3. a   4. c

4. USE YOUR READING SKILLS (p. 36)

1. c   2. a, b, c, d

6. UNDERSTAND THE READING

Exercise A (p. 38)

1. T   2. F   3. T   4. T   5. F

Exercise B (p. 38)

1, 3, 6

7. WORK WITH VOCABULARY

Exercise A (p. 39)

1. b   2. d   3. c   4. a

Exercise B (p. 39)

1. successful
2. success
3. succeed
4. successful
5. succeed
6. success

9. WORDS YOU NEED (p. 41)

1. d   2. b   3. f   4. a   5. c   6. e

10. USE YOUR READING SKILLS (p. 41)

1. b, c   2. a, c, e

12. UNDERSTAND THE READING

Exercise A (p. 43)

1. a job counselor
2. Find the right job.
3. should
4. should

Exercise B (p. 43)

1. her/Ana
2. them/ads
3. It/resume
4. they/employers,
5. them/employees

15. USE YOUR READING SKILLS

Exercise A (p. 44)

1. millions   2. immigrants

Exercise B (p. 44)

1. a   2. b

16. READ STORY A

Focus Questions (p. 45)

1. to give people an easier way to get a mattress; to start a new kind of company
2. people could call the company at any time of the day or night and order a mattress; the company could deliver a mattress to people's homes very quickly; he didn't need a store, so he could sell mattresses at a low price

16. READ STORY B

Focus Questions (p. 46)

1. she wanted to have her own house
2. she decided to make a plan and follow it to her dream; she worked very hard; she passed the high school equivalency exam; she found two jobs; every month, she saved a little more money

17. THINK AND SHARE

Organize Your Thoughts

Napoleon Barragan (p. 47)

1969/ moved to the U.S.; 1975/ opened their own furniture store; 1976/ started a new kind of company; 2000/ selling millions of mattresses every year; Today/ business is doing even better

Dorothea Sandiford (p. 47)

1970/ moved to the U.S.; 1985/ had enough money to buy a house; 1993/ started a day care business in her house; Today/ still runs her day care business

Share Your Ideas (p. 47)

hard work, a positive attitude, an idea, a dream, a plan, a better education

18. REFLECT ON: Success

Exercise B (p. 48)

1. he is in college
2. he worked very hard
3. his teachers, friends and family helped him

Unit 4 Keeping Calm

2. BUILD YOUR READING SKILLS

Introduction

Exercise B (p. 50)

It is in context.

Practice Understanding Vocabulary in Context
Exercise A (p. 51)

facial expressions/ faces; universal/ world; frown/ sadness, anger

3. WORDS YOU NEED (p. 52)

1. approaches   3. deal with
2. calm down   4. harmful

4. USE YOUR READING SKILLS

Exercise A (p. 52)

1. b   2. a, c, d, e

Exercise B (p. 52)

1. people express their anger in a very strong way
2. people keep their anger inside
3. people calm down and think about their anger
4. teaches people to manage or control their anger

5. UNDERSTAND THE READING

Exercise A (p. 54)

1. a, 2. b, 3. a, b,   4. c

Exercise B (p. 54)

1. T 2. T 3. T 4. F 5. F 6. T

7. WORK WITH VOCABULARY

Exercise A (p. 55)

1. a 2. c 3. d. 4. b

Exercise B (p. 55)

1. useful 2. helpful 3. harmful

8. GET READY TO READ ABOUT

Exercise B (p. 56)

June 7/ Listen to the other person. Don't interrupt.

June 14/ Think of solutions, not problems. Ask for advice.

June 21/ Think in a slow and careful way. Breathe deeply.

10. USE YOUR READING SKILLS

Exercise A (p. 57)

1. c 2. a, e

Exercise B (p. 57)

1. feel a little uncomfortable
2. don't form an opinion about a situation too quickly
3. looked at the wall for a long time

12. UNDERSTAND THE READING

Exercise A (p. 59)

1. jumping to conclusions
2. keeping calm
3. angry
4. staring at the wall

5. "He's not paying attention."
6. taking notes
7. embarrassed

Exercise B (p. 59)

1. she didn't follow her own advice; she thought the student wasn't paying attention; she didn't know the student was taking notes

13. WORK WITH VOCABULARY (p. 59)

1. a 2. b 3. c

14. GET READY TO READ AND SHARE

Exercise B (p. 60)

chart answers for women: girl; daughter; woman; female

chart answers for men: boy; son; man; male

15. USE YOUR READING SKILLS

Exercise A (p. 60)

1. yes   2. childhood

Exercise B (p. 60)

1. a 2. b

16. READ PART A

Focus Questions (p. 61)

1. don't cry; don't feel afraid hurt or sad; anger and fighting are masculine
2. fear, hurt, or sadness are difficult; anger is easier
3. positive side: men are often more comfortable expressing feelings of anger
   negative side: it is not helpful to yell and throw things; it is not healthy to keep feelings such as fear, hurt, or sadness inside

16. READ PART B

Focus Questions (p. 62)

1. it's OK to express emotions; anger is not a nice emotion and girls should always be nice; anger and fighting are not feminine
2. fear, hurt, or sadness are easy; anger is difficult
3. positive side/ they are more comfortable expressing fear, sadness, and many other emotions; negative side/ some women have difficulty expressing anger, and that is not healthy

17. THINK AND SHARE

Organize Your Thoughts (p. 63)
Chart A

anger and fighting; to cry or feel

afraid, hurt, or sad; anger; fear, hurt or sadness

Chart B

to express emotions; anger and fighting; fear, hurt, or sadness; anger

Chart A and B

to learn when anger is helpful; to learn to express their anger in helpful ways

18. REFLECT ON: Keeping Calm

Exercise B (p. 64)

1. because he was driving home from work and there was so much traffic
2. yes, she did; she decided not to drive and to take the bus; when she's not driving, she's not angry

Unit 5 The Business of Beauty

2. BUILD YOUR READING SKILLS

Practice Previewing Headlines (p. 67)
2, 3, 4

3. WORDS YOU NEED (p. 68)

1. e 2. a 3. b 4. c 5. d

4. USE YOUR READING SKILLS

Exercise A (p. 68)

1. c 2. b

Exercise B (p. 68)

1. did 2. changed

6. UNDERSTAND THE READING

Exercise A (p. 70)

1. b 2. e 3. a 4. c 5. d

Exercise B (p. 70)

1. thin   4. television
2. short   5. make-up
3. cosmetics   6. ideal

7. WORK WITH VOCABULARY

Exercise A (p. 71)

1. popular   3. cosmetics
2. short   4. make-up

Exercise B (p. 71)

1. e 2. c 3. d 4. a 5. b

8. GET READY TO READ ABOUT

Exercise A (p. 72)

1. False: Petite models are not tall, and "plus" models are not thin.
2. True
3. True
4. False: Modeling school can be useful, but it isn't necessary.

5. False: Modeling involves a lot of hard work.

Exercise B (p. 72)

1. g 2. c 3. b 4. d 5. i 6. a
7. h 8. e 9. f

9. WORDS YOU NEED (p. 73)

career/job; model/stands and moves to show clothing; portfolio/photographs from modeling jobs; agent/person can find work for you

10. USE YOUR READING SKILLS

Exercise A (p 73)

a

Exercise B (p. 73)

c, d, e

12. UNDERSTAND THE READING

Exercise A (p. 75)

1. e 2. c 3. d 4. a 5. b

13. WORK WITH VOCABULARY (p. 75)

1. c 2. f 3. e 4. b 5. d 6. a

15. USE YOUR READING SKILLS

Exercise A (p. 76)

1. it is becoming easier, cheaper and more popular with men
2. Alain Duchamp, a businessman and job counselor; Raj Singh, a lawyer in public health

Exercise B (p. 76)

1. against   2. for

16. READ PART A

Focus Questions (p. 77)

1. health risks are the most important reason; after cosmetic surgery people sometimes look unnatural ; people want to look better but they look worse
2. men should accept their big nose; they should love their wrinkles; they should go outside and exercise; they should feel good about their healthy body; they shouldn't think so much about their looks

16. READ PART B

Focus Questions (p. 78)

1. cosmetic surgery today is easier, cheaper, and better; every year doctors improve their skills, and now risks are small
2. it helps people look better; when

people look better, they feel better; cosmetic surgery can help your career; it can give you an advantage; it can give you more hair, take away wrinkles and give you more confidence

Unit 6 Finding the Right Balance

1 GET READY TO READ ABOUT

Introduction

Exercise B (p. 82)

1. c 2. f 3. a 4. e 5. d 6. b

2. BUILD YOUR READING SKILLS

Exercise B (p. 83)

1. campgrounds in national parks; campgrounds in state parks; private campgrounds
2. the U.S. government
3. companies

3. WORDS YOU NEED (p. 84)

1. a 2. b 3. a 4. b

4. USE YOUR READING SKILLS

Exercise A (p. 84)

1. camping
2. recreational; tent; wilderness

6. UNDERSTAND THE READING

Exercise A (p. 86)

1. a 2. b, c 3. a, b 4. c 5. b

7. WORK WITH VOCABULARY

Exercise A (p. 87)

1. d 2. b 3. a 4. c 5. e

Exercise B (p. 87)

1. b 2. c 3. a

9. WORDS YOU NEED

Exercise A (p. 89)

1. b 2. a

Exercise B (p. 89)

1. a 2. c 3. c

10. USE YOUR READING SKILLS

Exercise A (p 89)

1. study habits   2. a, b, e

12. UNDERSTAND THE READING

Exercise A (p. 91)

1. c 2. a 3. c 4. b 5. a

13. WORK WITH VOCABULARY (p. 91)

1. d 2. c 3. b 4. a

15. USE YOUR READING SKILLS

Exercise A (p. 92)

1. no

Exercise B (p. 92)

1. she joined the Peace Corps; she went to Africa
2. they bought land in Montana to live on; they started a sanctuary for animals

16. READ STORY A

Focus Questions (p. 93)

1. she wasn't ready to sit at a desk all day every day; she wanted adventure
2. she taught physics; she helped repair buildings; she helped farmers build better farm equipment
3. she found a job with a small company; she works in an office, but also travels a lot

16. READ PART B

Focus Questions (p. 94)

1. their jobs were OK and they earned a lot of money, but they didn't feel satisfied
2. they care for animals
3. they feel satisfied; their lives finally have the right balance

18. REFLECT ON: Finding the Right Balance

Exercise B (p. 96)

1. the student stayed home a lot but wanted to go out and have fun; he/she wanted more friends; he/she was afraid to talk to people
2. the student went to acting class
3. he/she found new friends and is much more comfortable with people; he/she goes out with friends

Unit 7 That's Entertainment

2. BUILD YOUR READING SKILLS

Practice Asking Questions While You Read

Exercise A (p. 99)

1. b

3. WORDS YOU NEED (p. 100)

1. a 2. b 3. a 4. a 5. a

4. USE YOUR READING SKILLS

Exercise A (p. 100)

1. the effects of television
2. a. Surveys of TV Viewing Habits; b. The Positive Effects of TV; c.

The Negative Effects of TV
Exercise B (p. 100–101)
1. b   2. b   3. a

6. UNDERSTAND THE READING

Exercise A (p. 102)
1. e   2. d   3. b   4. a   5. c
Exercise B (p. 102)
1. c   2. b   3. b   4. b

7. WORK WITH VOCABULARY

Exercise A (p. 103)
1. b   2. a   3. e   4. c   5. d
Exercise B (p. 103)
1. entertainment   4. educational
2. balanced   5. informative
3. reality

8. GET READY TO READ ABOUT

Exercise B (p. 104)
1. b   2. a   3. d   4. c

9. WORDS YOU NEED

Exercise A (p. 105)
1. c   2. b   3. d   4. a

10. USE YOUR READING SKILLS

Exercise A (p. 105–106)
1. favorite activities in a small town
2. high school football; the county fair; the community theater
Exercise B (p. 105–106)
1. a   2. a.   3. a

12. UNDERSTAND THE READING

Exercise A (p. 107)
1. a   2. a   3. b   4. c

13. WORK WITH VOCABULARY
   (p. 107)

1. boring   3. opportunities
2. event   4. loses

15. USE YOUR READING SKILLS

Exercise A (p. 108)
1. many tourists come to Amity for vacation every summer, and the town doesn't want them to leave
2. a boat captain; to kill a shark
Exercise B (p. 108)
1. a   2. b

16. READ REVIEW B

Focus Questions (p. 109)
1. the special effects
2. you don't see the shark much
3. it's so much more than just a horror movie; you care about the characters, so you feel frightened for them

16. READ REVIEW B

Focus Questions (p. 110)
1. it has good suspense
2. the mechanical shark looks fake; the acting isn't very good; the characters aren't interesting; all of their actions and words are too predictable
3. a shark can't think

Unit 8 The Comforts of Home

WHAT DO YOU KNOW ABOUT HOMES IN THE UNITED STATES?

Exercise A (p. 113)
BR/ bedroom; BA/ bathroom; kit./ kitchen; LR/ living room; DR/ dining room; transp./ transportation

1. GET READY TO READ ABOUT

Exercise A (p. 114)

```
S H O W E R T J C R I K
S L U N B T A A R X Z G
T D Y L O U B C O U C H
I R E W I V L R B L L M
R E F R I G E R A T O R
O S A U D W H N G B S V
H S E G O E J T D D E T
S E C O O T O I L E T D
A R P N R W I N D O W P
F O C E I L I N G H U I
```

Living Room: ceiling, couch, door, light, rug, table, window

Bedroom: bed, ceiling, closet, couch, door, dresser, light, rug, table, window

Bathroom: ceiling, door, light, rug, shower, toilet, window

Kitchen: ceiling, door, light, oven, refrigerator, table, window

2. BUILD YOUR READING SKILLS

Introduction
Exercise B (p. 115)
scanning
Practice Scanning (p. 115)
Exercise A (p. 115)
1. Wright was born
2. Wright died
Exercise B (p. 115)
1. architect   2. Pennsylvania

3. WORDS YOU NEED (p. 116)

1. technology   3. monitor
2. simplify   4. environment

4. USE YOUR READING SKILLS

Exercise A (p. 116)
1. the house of the future
2. research, technology, and life for the house of the future
Exercise B (p. 116)
1. a group of architects showed their ideas for "The House of the Future" at Disneyland
2. the "house of the future" will be just another normal house
3. Massachusetts Institute of Technology
4. MIT

6. UNDERSTAND THE READING

Exercise A (p. 118)
1. ~~past~~/future
2. ~~wood~~/plastic
3. ~~two-bedroom~~/one-bedroom
4. ~~television technology~~/computer technology
5. ~~people~~/information
6. ~~young~~/senior

7. WORK WITH VOCABULARY

Exercise A (p. 119)
1. b   2. a   3. b   4. b
Exercise B (p. 119)
1. c   2. c   3. a

8. GET READ TO READ ABOUT

Exercise A (p. 120)
1. c   2. e   3. b   4. f
5. a   6. h   7. d   8. g

9. WORDS YOU NEED (p. 121)

1. b   2. d   3. c   4. a

10. USE YOUR READING SKILLS

Exercise A (p. 121)
1. inventions all around us
2. the can opener
Exercise B (p. 121)
1. Ezra Warner invented the can opener
2. the Arctic
3. 260 tons of extra turkey meat
4. air conditioning

12. UNDERSTAND THE READING

Exercise A (p. 123)
1. b   2. a   3. a   4. b
Exercise B (p. 123)
1. he added a wheel to the can opener
2. TV dinner

13. WORK WITH VOCABULARY
(p. 123)

1. frozen   3. froze
2. freezer   4. freeze

15. USE YOUR READING SKILLS

Exercise A (p. 124)

1. ordinary houses
2. unusual houses

Exercise B (p. 124)

1. it looks like a goose
2. it is a tree house
3. from 1935 to 1940
4. from 2001 to 2003

16. READ PART A

Focus Questions (p. 125)

1. a goose skeleton
2. nobody knows
3. the windows of the house are shaped like goose eggs; one end of the roof has a 15-foot-tall goose's head with blue headlights from a car for eyes; the other end has a 10-foot-tail; the house is round and has small trees around it, so it looks like a goose on a nest

16. READ PART B

Focus Questions (p. 126)

1. the tree house could be a good place for guests
2. the tree house could be a good place for guests; they could live in the tree house
3. it is a tree house; they built it 14 feet from the ground; they built a big deck with holes for the tree's branches; on the deck , the Lines have a hot tub; the mailing address is just "Tree House."

17. THINK AND SHARE

Organize Your Thoughts (p. 127)
The Mother Goose House: What?/a goose house; Who?/George and Ollie Stacy; Where?/Hazard, Kentucky; How?/an architect helped them, they built it from the design of a goose skeleton; Describe/ *(Answers vary.)*; Why?/ nobody knows; When?/1935-1940

The Treehouse: What?/a tree house; Who?/Will and Peggy Line; Where?/Wadena, Minnesota; How?/they did the work themselves; Describe/ *(Answers vary.)*; Why?/ it could be a good place for guests; When?/ 2001–2003

Teacher's Notes

The Thinking Behind *Read and Reflect*

Read and Reflect follows current second-language reading pedagogy by ensuring that students:

- activate their background knowledge before and while they read.
- learn and apply effective reading strategies.
- read silently and with a purpose.
- interact with the material while they read.
- check their comprehension of a text.
- analyze, synthesize, and/or evaluate the author's ideas.

The texts in *Read and Reflect* are adapted from or modeled after authentic texts, such as newspaper and magazine articles, Web pages, message boards, and brochures. This is done to give beginning-level students as real a reading experience as possible. To ensure a successful experience, the adaptation adjusts the vocabulary and grammar to match the students' level.

In *Read and Reflect*, students are encouraged to read silently because the reading of a text is intended to be a silent interaction between the reader and the text (except in the case of poetry or reading to an audience). Although reading an individual word or single sentence aloud can help students' comprehension, reading an entire text aloud does not increase students' reading proficiency and is not emphasized in this book.

The variety of vocabulary exercises in *Read and Reflect*, as well as the wealth of contextualized vocabulary in the texts, assist students in the development of active and passive vocabulary. Getting meaning from context is a key reading strategy. Right from the beginning, students are encouraged to determine the meaning of new words from context rather than relying on their dictionaries. While students are given the opportunity to work with a dictionary in some pre-reading activities, reliance on the dictionary *while* reading often prevents the experience from being fluent and effective. In addition, academic words (e.g., create, respond, design, etc.) are introduced in order to help students prepare for academic reading in their English and content-based classes.

Read and Reflect, Introductory Level, lays a foundation for the development of critical literacy by providing opportunities for students to consider and clarify their own opinions, attitudes and values in relation to the text.

Teaching from Read and Reflect

Read and Reflect provides instructional flexibility, allowing you to tailor the activities to your classroom setting and your students' needs. One need universal to all students is to understand the purpose of their learning. The "To the Student" page (p. vi) introduces the purpose of this series and provides suggestions to help students read better. You can also reinforce this concept in class and emphasize the goals of each unit before you teach it, and point out how students have met those goals at the end of the unit.

A Tour of the Unit

The unit tour below outlines the purpose of each type of activity and provides teaching suggestions.

OPENING PAGE

The goals on the opening page identify the unit's cultural theme and reading strategies. The cartoon or illustration on the page prompts students to think about and discuss what they already know about the theme of the unit.

Teaching Suggestions

- Go over the appropriate language and non-verbal behavior for stating opinions and agreeing or disagreeing with others, before having students engage in the discussion activities on this page.

- To ensure greater participation in discussions in the beginning-level classroom, give students time to think or write about their responses to discussion questions before they speak. Another way to ensure participation is to have one student respond to a question and have five or six other students create a chain of responses based on what the first student said. For example, if Jose says "People need money to succeed. What do you think, Pat?" Pat can say, "I agree with you. What do you think, Tanya?" Tanya may say, "I disagree. You can succeed with no money. What do you think, Mario?" etc.

GET READY TO READ

Before reading the first and second texts of the unit, students complete pre-reading activities that activate their prior knowledge about the reading topics. Students are exposed to key vocabulary in this section and in the Words You Need section that follows.

Teaching Suggestions

- One type of vocabulary activity in this section has students work in pairs or teams to discuss the meanings of words they know from a list of key vocabulary. Then they look up the words they don't know in a dictionary. Encourage students to ask other teams or pairs to define words they don't know before looking them up.

BUILD YOUR READING SKILLS

These activities introduce important reading skills such as previewing or scanning, and explain the strategies students can use to implement these skills. For example, looking for specific signals, such as numbers to find dates and capital letters to find names, is a strategy for scanning. Students are first introduced to the strategies in a visual way so that they can begin to understand them implicitly. Then they are given an explicit definition of the skill and an opportunity to practice the strategies. After students practice them, they apply the new reading strategies (as well as strategies from previous units) in the Use Your Reading Skills section that follows.

Teaching Suggestions

- Provide an example of the reading skill and strategies in the unit, before having students read about them. For example, for previewing, show students a large newspaper headline or picture and have them tell you what the newspaper article is about. For scanning, put a classified advertisement on the overhead projector or board and have students tell you the name of the product or the contact phone number. Name the strategy students are employing and explain the rationale for using it. Elicit situations in which students have used the same strategy.

WORDS YOU NEED

This section introduces key vocabulary students will find in the text that follows. These words will be reviewed and practiced in the Work with the Vocabulary section later in the unit. Many of them will also be recycled in future units.

Teaching Suggestions

- In these exercises, students are often asked to guess meanings of vocabulary they will encounter in the text. Ask students to check their guesses once they have had an opportunity to read the material. Then give them a chance to share with a partner or with the class whether they guessed correctly.

USE YOUR READING SKILLS

This section provides students an opportunity to apply the new reading strategies (as well as ones they have learned in other units) to the text they will be reading. All reading skills and strategies are recycled throughout the book in order to give students the maximum opportunity to learn and use the skills.

Teaching Suggestions

- Periodically review the strategies the students have learned. Ask students to monitor their use of these strategies in their reading outside of class and encourage students to identify the ways these strategies help their reading comprehension.

READ

The four theme-related texts in each unit help students deepen their understanding of the theme, read with greater comprehension, and internalize recycled vocabulary. The first text is typically an academic text such as an encyclopedia or textbook article. The second text is usually lighter in tone and often has a more conversational style; for example, an editorial or personal essay. The third and fourth texts are part of the Read and Share activity (see next page but may also be taught as independent texts).

Important vocabulary in the texts is either introduced in the pre-reading activities or presented in context. Difficult content words that are key to students' understanding, but that are not high frequency words, are glossed. Words that are not important to a general understanding of a text are left undefined and students can skip over them.

Teaching Suggestions

- To help students get the most meaning from their reading, show them how to use the glossaries on the page, and then ask them to read the text once silently. Tell them to read without looking up unknown words.

- Set a short time limit for students to read the text and answer the questions. A time limit requires students to finish at the same time so that they can begin their pair or group work simultaneously.

- Once students have read the text, have them work on the Understand the Reading questions. Encourage them to answer all the questions first and then go back to check their answers against the text. They can check in pairs or small groups. Explain that this procedure will help them evaluate how much of the text they understood.

- Once the processing questions have been answered and checked, you can read the text aloud to the class while they follow along silently. As you read, model some "think aloud" techniques, such as asking yourself the following types of questions aloud, *Is that true?* or *What is the author telling me?* This will help students understand the thinking processes used by effective readers.

- If time permits, allow students to read the text a third time, circling three words they want to add to their active vocabulary. Give students time to record these words and their definitions in a separate section of their notebooks.

UNDERSTAND THE READING

After reading the first and second text in each unit, students do exercises to check their comprehension and use their higher-level thinking skills to analyze or evaluate the information they read. The first time an exercise type is introduced in the book, a sample answer is given.

Teaching Suggestions

- For the first exercise of this section, encourage students to do the exercise individually, and then to look back at the text to check their answers with a partner or teammates.

- In this section, there is usually a second exercise, which is intended to help students think critically about the text. To ensure that every student has a chance to think about the topic, tell students to first answer the questions individually, and then discuss their answers with a partner, a small group, or the whole class.

- In order to help develop students' critical literacy, each text has brief introductory material identifying its source or the author's background. To help students develop critical literacy, ask them questions such as: *Why does the author include information from surveys?* (Unit 1, Text 1) or *Does an interview usually have facts or opinions?* (Unit 3, Text 2, or Unit 5, Text 2).

WORK WITH THE VOCABULARY

After reading the first and second text in each unit, students increase their active vocabulary through a variety of exercises. These include working with definitions, suffixes, word families, verb phrases, and context clues.

Teaching Suggestions

- Encourage students to keep a journal of vocabulary words including those presented in this section, the glossed words, and other words from the text. Then have students note each time they encounter these words in their reading outside of class.

- Recycle the words students learn in each unit in other class activities. This will increase the likelihood of new words becoming part of your students' active vocabulary.

READ AND SHARE

These four pages comprise a highly effective and communicative technique for developing reading proficiency. The Read and Share technique follows these steps:

GET READY TO READ AND SHARE

1. Students complete pre-reading and vocabulary activities related to the topic.

Use Your Reading Skills

2. Students read the introduction to the text they will read in Read A/B. They answer questions about it to ensure that they know what the text is about.

3. Students preview the two parts of the text in order to select one to read.

READ A/READ B

4. Students read the part of the text they chose with the purpose of learning new information and then sharing it with a partner.

5. When the class finishes reading, each student finds a partner who has read the same part of the text and they work in pairs to answer the focus questions relating to their text.

THINK AND SHARE
ORGANIZE YOUR THOUGHTS

6. In this section students work with the partner who read the same part of the text they did. Together they fill in a graphic organizer which helps them deepen their understanding of the reading.

Share Your Information

7. Students then work with another pair that has read the other part of the text. The pairs take turns sharing what they have read, using the graphic organizer to guide their presentation.

SHARE YOUR IDEAS

8. In small groups or as a whole class, students use what they have learned from the texts as well as their background knowledge and personal experience to respond to follow-up questions.

Teaching Suggestions

- Each time students do a Read and Share activity, remind them of the purpose for the activity. Tell students that during the Read and Share they will choose one of two parts of the same text and work with a partner to answer questions about the text. Once they understand the most important ideas in their text, they will share these ideas with a pair of students who read the other text.

- This activity works best if students choose their own text; however, this can be tricky if most students prefer one text over another (20 students pick A, 3 pick B). If you prefer not to leave the selection to chance, you can assign A/B roles to students.

- To give students an additional reading opportunity, you can assign the other text as an in-class activity or as homework.

- From time to time you may want to have all students read the A and B texts sequentially instead of as a Read and Share activity. In this case, have students read one text and answer the corresponding focus questions. It may be helpful to put the focus questions for the selected text on the board or overhead. Then repeat the process for the other text.

REFLECT

Students first read an example of a student response to the ideas presented in the unit. Next they answer comprehension questions about the sample response, and finally write their own response using guided questions.

Teaching Suggestions

- The writing activity is guided, so it can be assigned as homework; however, the pre-writing activity allows for discussion about the writing topic and is most effective if done in class.